THE MARRIAGE RING

"Setting aside all other considerations,
I will endeavor to know the truth
and yield to that."

Tillotson

"The secret of happiness lies folded
up in the leaves of the Bible."

THE
MARRIAGE
RING

or
How to Make Home Happy

John Angell James

1785-1859, English Nonconformist Preacher

2010 Edition
Modernized and edited from the 1842 Edition

Hail & Fire
www.hailandfire.com

"The Marriage Ring, or How to Make Home Happy," from the writings of John Angell James, appended with a sermon newly entitled "Right to Divorce & Remarriage in the Case of Adultery," by John Owen, is herein modernized, edited, and republished with newly added footnotes by Hail & Fire.

ISBN-10 0982804326
ISBN-13 978-0-9828043-2-2

Hail & Fire is a resource for Reformed and Gospel Theology in the works, exhortations, prayers, and apologetics of those who have maintained the Gospel and expounded upon the Scripture as the Eternal Word of God and the sole authority in Christian doctrine.

Visit us online at: www.hailandfire.com

*For those who hunger and thirst
after righteousness*

CONTENTS

BONUS SERMON:

Right to Divorce & Remarriage in the Case of Adultery

"By manifestation of the truth commending ourselves to every man's conscience in the sight of God."
2 Corinthians 4:2

HAIL & FIRE

Hail & Fire is a resource for Reformed and Gospel
Theology in the works, exhortations, prayers,
and apologetics of those who have
maintained the Gospel and
expounded upon the
Scripture
as the Eternal Word of God
and the sole authority in Christian doctrine.

For the edification of those who hold the Gospel
in truth and for the examination of every
conscience, Hail & Fire reprints
and republishes, in print
and online,
Christian,
Puritan, Reformed
and Protestant sermons and
exhortative works; Protestant and
Catholic polemical and apologetical works;
Bibles histories, martyrologies, and eschatological works.

Visit us online: www.hailandfire.com

PREFACE
from the 1842 Edition

PREFACE
from the 1842 Edition

*"Pure, open, prosperous love,
That, pledged on earth and sealed above,
Grows in the world's approving eyes,
In friendship's smile and home's caress,
Collecting all the heart's sweet ties
Into one knot of happiness!"*

This little book, intended as a manual for those just entering the marriage state, was principally selected from the works of an author beloved and esteemed for his many practical writings, and who has very justly remarked:

"It is an unquestionable truth, that if a man is not happy at home, he cannot be happy anywhere; and he who is happy there, need be miserable nowhere. 'It is the place in all the world I love most,' said the interesting author of the 'Task,' when speaking of home. And he may be felicitated who can say the same. Any attempt, however feeble, to render the domestic circle what it ever should be—a scene of comfort—is at least benevolent. The secret of happiness lies folded up in the leaves of the Bible and is carried in the heart of true religion.

The author knows of no other way to happiness and, therefore, does not profess to teach any other. Let the two parties in wedded life be believers in Christ Jesus and partake themselves of the peace that surpasses understanding. Let them, when they become a father and a mother, bring up their children in the fear of God. And if happiness is to be found on earth, it will be enjoyed within the hallowed circle of a family thus united by love and sanctified by grace."

Most of the works published on this subject have been of a light and trifling character, but the compiler of this book has aimed to present such a work as might be deemed a suitable offering from the hand of a pastor or a Christian friend.

CHAPTER 1
Forming the Marriage Union

CHAPTER 1
Forming the Marriage Union

"Happy they! The happiest of their kind!
Whom gentler stars unite; and in one fate
Their hearts, their fortunes, and their being blend."

It must be evident to all, that marriage is a step of incalculable importance, which should never be taken without the greatest consideration and the utmost caution. If the duties of this state are so numerous and so weighty and if the right discharge of these obligations, as well as the happiness of our whole life and even our safety for eternity, depend, as they necessarily must, in no small measure upon the choice we make of a husband or wife, then let sound reason determine with what deliberation we should advance to such a relationship. It is obvious that no decision we make during our entire earthly existence requires more of the exercise of a calm judgment than this one does. Yet, observation proves just how rarely judgment is allowed to give counsel and how commonly the imagination and the passions settle the matter.

A very great portion of the misery and crime with which society is depraved and afflicted is the result of ill-formed marriages. To use the beautiful language of another, *"those who enter the marriage state cast a die of the greatest contingency, and yet of the greatest interest in the world, next to the last throw for eternity. Life or death, felicity or a lasting sorrow, are in the power of marriage. A woman indeed ventures the most, for she has no sanctuary to retire to from an evil husband; she must dwell upon her sorrow, which her own folly has produced; and she is the more burdened under it, because her tormentor has warrant of prerogative. The woman may complain to God, as subjects do of tyrant princes, but otherwise, she has no appeal in the causes of unkindness. And though the man can run from many hours of sadness, yet he must return to it again; and when he sits among his neighbors, he remembers the objection that lies in his bosom, and he sighs deeply."*

If, however, it were merely the comfort of the married pair themselves that was concerned, it would be a matter of less consequence and a stake of less value, but the wellbeing of a family, not only for this world but also for the next, and equally so, the wellbeing of their descendants, even to a distant period in the future, depends upon this union. In the ardor of passion, few are disposed to listen to the counsels of prudence and perhaps there is no advice, generally speaking, more thrown away, than that which is offered on the subject of marriage.

Most people, especially if they are already attached to a particular individual, although they have not committed themselves by any promise or even a declaration, will go on in their pursuit, blinded by love, to the indiscretion of their choice; or, desperately determined, in spite of their knowledge of that indiscretion, to accomplish their purpose if possible. Upon such individuals, reasoning often proves wasted and they must be left to gain wisdom in the only way that some will acquire it—

through painful experience. To others, who may yet be disengaged and disposed to hearken to the language of advice, the following remarks are offered.

Consulting the Advice of Parents

In the affair of marriage, be guided by the advice of parents and guardians. Parents have no right to select for you—nor should you select for yourself without consulting them. Just how far they are vested with the authority to prohibit you from marrying a person whom they disapprove is a point of casuistry, which is very difficult to determine.

If you are of age and able to provide for yourselves or are likely to be well provided for by those to whom you are about to be united, it is a question whether your parents can do anything more than advise and persuade. However, until you are of age, they have a positive authority to forbid and it is an undutiful act in you to form relationships without their knowledge and to carry on such relationships against their prohibitions.[1]

Their objections, I admit, should always be founded upon reason and not upon caprice or pride. For, where this is the case and the children are of full age and are guided in their choice by prudence, piety, and affection, they certainly may and must be left to decide for themselves. When, however, parents rest their objections on sufficient grounds and show plain and palpable reasons for prohibiting a relationship, then it is the manifest duty of sons and especially of daughters, to give up that relationship.[2] Very seldom does that

---

1. "Children, obey your parents in the Lord: for this is right. Honor your father and mother, which is the first commandment with promise; that it may be well with you, and you may live long on the earth." Ephesians 6:1-2.
2. "Trust in the Lord and do good." Psalm 37:3. "Seek first the kingdom

union prove to be anything but a source of misery on which the frown of an affectionate and wise father and mother fall from the beginning; for God seems to rise up in judgment and to support the parents' authority by confirming their displeasure with his own.

Importance of Mutual Affection

In every case, marriage should be formed upon the basis of mutual affection. If there is no love before marriage, it cannot be expected that there should be any after it. Lovers, as all are supposed to be who are looking forward to this union, without love, have no right to expect happiness and the coldness of indifference is soon likely, in their case, to be changed into aversion. There should be personal attachment. For, if there is anything, even in the exterior, that excites disgust, the banns are forbidden by the very voice of nature.

I do not say that beauty of countenance or elegance of form is necessary—by no means, a pure and strong attachment has often existed in the absence of these. And I will not take it upon myself to determine whether it is absolutely impossible to love deformity. However, we should certainly not unite ourselves with it unless we can love it or, at least, are so enamored with the fascination of mental qualities that are united with it, as to lose sight of the body in the charms of the mind, heart, and manners. All I contend for is this—that to proceed to marriage in spite of absolute dislike and revulsion is irrational, base, and sinful.

of God and his righteousness; and all these things shall be added to you." Matthew 6:33. "Be anxious for nothing; but in everything by prayer and supplication with thanksgiving let your requests be made known to God. And the peace of God, which passes all understanding, shall keep your hearts and minds through Christ Jesus." Philippians 4:6-7.

Love should respect the mind as well as the body. For, to be attached to an individual simply on the ground of beauty is to fall in love with a doll, a statue, or a picture. Such an attachment is lust or fancy but certainly not rational affection. If we love the body but do not love the mind, heart, and manners, our regard is placed upon the inferior part of the person and therefore, only upon that which through disease may, by the next year, be a very different thing than what it is at first. Nothing fades so soon as beauty. It is like the delicate bloom of an attractive fruit, which, if there is nothing agreeable underneath it, will be thrown away in disgust when that is brushed off, and it will be thrown away by the very hand of him that plucks it.

It is so commonly remarked as to be proverbial, that the charms of the mind increase by acquaintance, while those of the exterior are diminished by acquaintance. While the charms of the mind easily reconcile us to a plain countenance, the charms of the exterior excite by the power of contrast, a distaste for the insipidness, ignorance, and heartlessness with which they are united—like gaudy scentless flowers growing in a desert. Instead of determining to stake our happiness on the act of gathering these flowering weeds to place them in our bosom, let us ask how they will look in a few years from now or how they will adorn and bless our habitation. Let us ask if the understanding, united with that countenance, render its owner fit to be my companion and the instructor of my children? Will that temper patiently bear with my weaknesses, kindly consult my tastes, and affectionately study my comfort? Will those manners please me in solitude, as well as in society? Will those habits render my dwelling pleasant to me and to my friends? We must carefully consider these matters and hold our passions back so that we may take counsel with our judgment and suffer reason to talk with us in quiet contemplation.

Such then, is the love on which marriage should be formed—love of the whole person: love of the mind, heart, and manners, as well as the countenance and form. Love tempered with respect. For this is the only attachment that is likely to survive the charms of novelty, the spoliation of disease, and the influence of time, and to support the tender sympathies and exquisite sensibilities of the conjugal state. This attachment is able to render man and wife, to the verge of extreme old age, what they should be, the help and the comfort of each other, according to the intention of him who instituted the marriage union.

Young people should be extremely careful not to let the persuasions of others, the impulse of their own covetousness, their anxiety to be their own masters, or the ambition for secular glory, induce them into entering a marriage to which they are not drawn by the solicitations of a pure and virtuous love. What will a large house, expensive furniture, luxury transportation, and fashionable entertainments do for their possessor in the absence of connubial love? "Is it for these baubles, these toys," exclaims the miserable heart as it awakens, alas, too late, in some sad scene of domestic woe: "Is it for this that I have bartered away myself, my happiness, and my honor?"

> "How ill the scenes that offer rest,
> And hearts that cannot rest, agree!"

Oh, there is such a sweetness, a charm, and a power to please in pure and mutual affection, even if it is cherished in the humblest abode and maintained amidst the poorest circumstances, and has to contend with many difficulties. The elegance and splendor of worldly grandeur, compared with this, are as the beauty of an Eastern palace compared to a shady place in the Garden of Eden.[1] Let a man nobly determine *to earn his daily bread by the sweat of his brow*[2] and to find his daily task sweetened by the thought that it is for the woman he loves, rather than travel about in coveted style and live a life of luxurious indolence and misery with a woman he does not love. Likewise, let the other sex just as nobly and heroically determine to trust to their own energies and especially to a gracious Providence, rather than marry without affection for the sake of a settlement.[3]

There is, then, another error committed by some, who, having been disappointed in a relationship which they had hoped to form, become reckless for the future and, in a temper of mind bordering upon revenge, accept the first individual who presents themselves, whether they love them or not.[4] This is the height of folly and is such an act of suicidal violence against their own peace, as can neither be described nor reprobated in sufficiently strong terms. This is to act like the enraged scorpion and to turn their sting upon themselves, and in a rash act of passion to sacrifice their own happiness to folly.

Consulting the Rules of Prudence

Marriage should always be contracted with the strictest regard to the rules of prudence.[5] Discretion is a virtue

---

1. "Better is a little with the fear of the Lord, than great treasure with trouble. Better is a dinner of herbs where love is, than a stalled ox with hatred." Proverbs 15:16-17.

2. Genesis 3:19.

3. *Settlement:* that which is appointed for her personal maintenance and domestic state.

4. "Be anxious for nothing; but in everything by prayer and supplication with thanksgiving let your requests be made known to God. And the peace of God, which passes all understanding, shall keep your hearts and minds through Christ Jesus." Philippians 4:6-7.

5. "The prudent man looks well to his ways." Proverbs 14:15.

at which none but fools will laugh.[1] In reference to no other subject is discretion more frequently set aside and despised than in that which, of all that can be mentioned, needs most its sober counsels. For love to be seen standing attentive at the oracle of wisdom is thought, by some romantic and heedless individuals, to be a thing altogether out of place. If they alone were concerned, they might be left to their folly to be punished by its fruits, but imprudent marriages, as we have already considered, spread far and wide their bad consequences and also convey those consequences to posterity.

Our understanding is given to us to control our passions and our imagination. Those, who, in an affair of such great consequence as choosing a companion for life, set aside the testimony of the understanding and listen only to the advice of the passions and the imagination, have, in that instance at least, forfeited the character of a rational being and sunk to the level of those creatures who are wholly governed by appetite unchecked by reason. Prudence would prevent so much human misery if it were allowed to guide the conduct of mankind. In the business before us, it would allow no one to marry until they had a prospect of supporting themselves. It is perfectly obvious to me that the present generation of young people are not distinguished by a discretion of this kind. They are too much in haste to enter the conjugal state and place themselves at the heads of families before they have any rational hope of being able to support them. Almost as soon as they arrive at the age of manhood, whether they are in business or not and before they have ascertained whether their business will succeed or not, they look around for a wife and make a hasty and perhaps an injudicious selection. Let

---

1. "Discretion shall preserve you, understanding shall keep you." Proverbs 2:11.

young people exercise their reason and their foresight or, if they will not and are determined to rush into the expense of housekeeping before they have resources to meet the expenses, let them hear, in spite of the siren song of their imagination, the voice of faithful warning and prepare to eat the bitter herbs of useless regrets, for many a long and weary year after the nuptial feast has passed away.

Extreme Differences in Age & Rank

Prudence forbids all unequal marriages. There should be an equality as near as may be in age. How unnatural and how odious is it to see a young man fastened to a piece of antiquity, so as to perplex strangers in determining whether he is living with a wife or a mother! No one will give the woman in the one case or the man in the other, the credit of marrying for love and the world will be ill-disposed enough to the match. One can hardly help joining in the censoring of such marriages as mere pecuniary spectacles, for, generally speaking, the older party in the union is a rich one and generally they carry a scourge in their wallet by which they maintain power over the other. Thus, a fortune has often been a misfortune for both.

Equality of rank is desirable or as near to it as possible. It is much less perilous for a rich man to look below his status in society for a wife, than it is for a rich woman to look below hers for a husband. He can much more easily raise his companion to his own level, than she can and society will much more readily accommodate themselves to his choice, than to hers. Much of the happiness of the conjugal state depends upon the relatives of the parties, so that, if the marriage has offended them and if it has degraded them, how much bitterness is in their power to throw into the cup of marital enjoyment! Many a wife has carried to her grave the sting inflicted upon her peace by the insults of her husband's friends and family and, in all such cases, he will have received a part of that venom also.

Special Caution for Ministers

To my brethren in the ministry I do recommend and recommend with an earnestness that I have no language sufficiently emphatic to express, the greatest caution in this most delicate and important affair in their own lives. In their case, the effects of an imprudent marriage are felt in the church of the living God. If the wives of deacons are to be *"grave, not slanderers, sober, faithful in all things,"*[1] then what less can be required of the wives of pastors? *"A bishop must be blameless ... one who rules his own house well, having his children in subjection with all gravity. For if a man does not know how to rule his own house, how shall he take care of the church of God?"*[2] How can he exhibit in the governing of his own house the beautiful order and harmony which should prevail in every Christian family and especially in every minister's house, without the intelligent and industrious cooperation of his wife? Moreover, how can this be expected if he should marry one who has no intelligence or industry? Not only the comfort but much of the character of a minister depends upon his wife and, what is of still greater consequence, much of his usefulness.

Uniformity of Faith & Beliefs

Marriage should always be formed with a due regard to the dictates of religion.[3] A pious person should not

---

1. 1 Timothy 3:11.   2. 1 Timothy 3:2-5.
3. "'Seek first the kingdom of God and his righteousness and all these things shall be added to you.' - 'Whatever you do in word or in deed, do all in the name of the Lord Jesus.' - 'Therefore, whether you eat or drink,

marry anyone who is not also pious. It is not desirable to be united to an individual even of a different denomination who, as a point of conscience, attends their own place of worship. It is not pleasant on a Sunday morning to separate and to go, one to one place of worship and the other to another. The most delightful walk that a holy couple can take is to the house of God in each other's company and when, in reference to the elevated themes of redemption and the realities of eternity, to take sweet counsel together. No one would willingly give this up, but, oh, to walk separately in a still more important and dreadful sense! To part at the place where the two roads to eternity branch off, the one to heaven and the other to hell, and for the believer *"to travel on to glory, with the awful consciousness, that the other party is journeying to perdition!"* This is indeed terrible and it is sufficient in itself to be the occasion of no small diminishing of conjugal happiness.

Marrying Only in the Lord

If, however, only the comfort of the two parties were concerned, it would be a matter of less consequence, but it is a matter of conscience and an affair in which we have no option. *"She is at liberty to marry whom she will,"* says the apostle, speaking on the case of a

---

or whatever you do, do all to the glory of God. Give no offence, either to the Jews or to the Gentiles or to the church of God.' - 'For you were bought with a price, therefore glorify God in your body and in your spirit, which are God's,' (Matthew 6:33; Colossians 3:17; 1 Corinthians 10:31-32 and 6:20). These general maxims should govern all your actions. How much is it to be lamented then, that, in the article of marriage, so little regard is paid to the law of Christ by those who profess to be his subjects! Many an ardent youth will say, 'Will I, in this relationship, please my own taste? Will I gratify the wishes of my parents? Will I receive a fund of domestic comfort? Will it enlarge my capital for the purposes of trade and commerce? Will it raise me higher in the state of society? Will it advance my respectability and influence in the city?' But a Christian will more earnestly inquire:

widow, but *"only in the Lord."*[1] Now, although this was said in reference to a female, all the reasons of the law belong with equal force to the other sex. This appears to me to be not only advice but law, and as such, it is as binding upon the conscience as any other law that we find in the Word of God. The incidental manner in which this injunction occurs is, as has been very properly remarked, to the truthful reader of Scripture, the strongest confirmation of the rule in all cases where marriage is a prospect and was not contracted prior to the conversion of one party.

Do Not Be Unequally Yoked

As to the other passage, where the apostle commands us to *"not be unequally yoked together with unbelievers,"*[2] it does not apply to marriage except by inference, but to church fellowship or rather to association and conduct in general, in reference to which, professing Christians are not to be unequally yoked together with unbelievers. And, if this is improper in regard to other matters, how much more improper is it in that relationship which has so powerful an influence over our character as well as our happiness! For a Christian, then, to marry an individual who is not decidedly and evidently a pious believer is in direct opposition to the Word of God.

'Will this relationship glorify God? Am I likely to be a helpmeet to a pious woman? May I hope to be essentially benefited in the interests of my own soul? Will it enable me to be more useful in all the departments of life? Have I seriously prayed for divine direction in my choice, remembering, that, "a prudent wife is from the Lord," (Proverbs 19:14). Have I combined watchfulness with prayer, knowing that diligence and dependence should always be found together? If they were now on earth, could I comfortably invite Jesus himself and his apostles to the wedding?'" W.N., *On Marriage, Addressed to Young Christians.*

1. 1 Corinthians 7:39.   2. 2 Corinthians 6:14.

And as Scripture is against it, so also is reason; for how *"can two walk together, except they be agreed?"*[1] A difference of taste in minor matters is an impediment in the way of domestic comfort but to be opposed to each other on the all important subject of religion is a risk which no considerate person should be induced to incur upon any considerations. How can the higher purposes of the domestic constitution be answered, when one of the parents does not have the spiritual qualifications necessary to accomplish them? How can the work of religious education be conducted and the children be trained up *"in the nurture and admonition of the Lord?"*[2]

And as it respects individual and personal assistance in religious matters, do we not all want helps instead of hindrances?[3] A Christian should make everything bend to religion, but allow religion to bend to nothing. This is the one thing that is needful, to which everything else should be subordinate and, surely, to place out of consideration the affairs of our eternal salvation in so important an affair as marriage, shows either that the religion of a person who acts this way is but profession or that it will soon likely become so.[4]

---

1. Amos 3:3.   2. Ephesians 6:4.

3. "The righteous is more excellent than his neighbor, but the way of the wicked seduces them." Proverbs 12:26.

4. "Remarkably worthy of notice appears the solemn charge which the Lord gave to Israel concerning the Canaanites: 'You shall not make marriages with them. You shall not give your daughter to his son, nor take his daughter for your son. For they will turn your son away from following me, that they may serve other gods: so will the anger of the Lord be kindled against you, and destroy you suddenly,' (Deuteronomy 7:3-4). These admonitions being disregarded, from unhallowed marriages flowed all the miseries of the numerous captivities to which the tribes of Israel were subjected." W.N., On Marriage, Addressed to Young Christians.

Earnest Prayer for Direction

No one should contemplate the prospect of such a weighty union as marriage without the greatest and most serious deliberation, nor without the most earnest prayer to God for direction. Prayer, however, to be acceptable to the Almighty, should be sincere and should be presented with a real desire to know and do his will.[1] I believe that many act towards God as they do towards their friends: they make up their minds and *then* they ask to be directed. They have some doubts and very often strong doubts about the propriety of the step they are about to take, but these are gradually dissipated by their supplications, until they have prayed themselves into a conviction that they are quite right in the decision, which they have, in fact, already made.

To pray for direction in an affair that we *know* to be in opposition to God's Word and on which we have already resolved to act is to add hypocrisy to rebellion.[2] If there is reason to believe that the individual that solicits a Christian woman to unite herself to him in marriage, is not truly pious, what need does she have of praying to God to be directed regarding the match? None.[3] This is to ask the Almighty God to be permitted to do that which he has forbidden us to do.

Considerations for a Second Marriage

In the case of widows and widowers, especially where there is a family, peculiar prudence is necessary. I have

---

1. "Not my will, but yours, be done." Luke 22:42.

2. "To venture upon the occasion of sin, and then to pray, 'Do not lead us into temptation,' is one and the same as to thrust your finger into the fire, and then to pray that it might not be burned." Thomas Brooks, Precious Remedies Against Satan's Devices (1676).

3. "Go from the presence of a foolish man, when you do not perceive in him the lips of knowledge." Proverbs 14:7.

known instances in which such persons have sacrificed all their own tastes and predilections and have made their selection with exclusive reference to their children. Such a sacrifice is indeed generous, but it may become a question whether it is discreet. It is to place one's own comfort and even character in danger to some degree and, neither comfort or character can be lost without doing serious mischief to the very children whose interests have been so heroically considered. This, however, is an error much more rare and venial than that of the opposite extreme: for example, how unseemly and inconsiderate is it for a man in his sixties to bring home a young wife and place her over daughters who are older than she is, and to introduce into the family circle aunts and uncles younger than some of the nephews and nieces. Rare is the case in which such inexpedient relationships are formed without the authors of them losing much of their own reputation and destroying much of the comfort of their families. Let not such men wonder, if their daughters from the first marriage are driven from their home by the consequences of the second and are led to form imprudent matches, to which they were urged by the force of parental example and by the consequences of parental folly.

In the selection of a second companion for life, where the first was eminent in talents or virtues, much care should be taken that there is no great and striking inferiority in the second. For, in such a case,

> *"Busy, meddling memory,*
> *In barbarous succession, musters up*
> *The past endearments of their softer hours;"*

which form a contrast ever present and ever painful. The man that has know by experience the joys of a happy marriage cannot imagine the ills of an imprudent one aggravated by the power of comparison. Let him that has thus known the joys of a happy marriage beware how he exposes himself to such helpless, hopeless misery.

Best Interests of Children

Due care should also be exercised in reference to the interest of children from a first marriage. Has the woman, who is to be selected as stepmother, that principle, that prudence, that self-control, that good temper, which, if she herself becomes a mother, will help her to conceal her partialities, (for to absolutely and entirely suppress such partialities is impossible, since it is unnatural) and to seem no less kind to her adopted offspring than to her own? That man acts most cruelly and plays a most wicked part towards the memory of his first wife, who does not provide for her children a kind and judicious friend in his second wife. Let me become the advocate of fatherless or motherless children and entreat for the sake of both the living and the dead, a due regard to the comfort of these orphans.

Taking on the Responsibility of Stepchildren

Nor should less deliberation be exercised by the party who is about to take on or is invited to take on the care of another person's children. Have they love enough for the parent to bear the burden of caring for his children for his sake? Have they kindness enough and discretion enough for such a situation and for such an office? There is little difficulty when the children are lovely in person and amiable in temperament, but when they have no personal attractions, no charms of mind, and no endearments of character, then is the time to consider the truth of the saying, *"a wife may be supplied, a mother cannot."* The man or the woman that can act a parent's part towards a froward and unlovely child, must have more than nature—for this belongs only to a real parent. They must have principle and kindness, and they will need grace. Let those who are invited to take upon themselves the superintendence of an existing family, ask themselves if they possess the requisites for the comfortable and satisfactory discharge of its duties. Let them inquire whether it is likely that they can be happy in such a situation themselves. And, if not, they would do better not to enter it, as their unhappiness would inevitably fill the whole family with misery.

Prepare for the Duties of Marriage

It cannot be sufficiently deplored that all suitable preparation for the marriage state is typically set aside for the busy activities of vanity, which, in fact, are but as dust on the balance of conjugal destiny. Every thought and anticipation, and anxiety is too often absorbed in the selection of a house and furniture, and in matters still more insignificant and frivolous. How common is it for a woman to spend hours, day after day and week after week, conversing with her dressmaker, debating and discussing the color, form, and material in which she is to shine forth in nuptial splendor; as if the object was to appear a merry and fashionable bride, rather than to be a good and happy wife! This time should be employed in meditating the eventful step that is about to fix for life her destiny and that of her intended husband.

> *"Joy, serious, and sublime,*
> *Such as does nerve the energies of prayer,*
> *Should swell the bosom, when a maiden's hand,*
> *Filled with life's dewy flowerets, girds on*

> *That harness, which the ministry of death*
> *Alone unlooses, but whose fearful power*
> *May stamp the sentence of eternity."*

"Study," said an old author, *"the duties of marriage before you enter into it. There are crosses to be borne, there are snares to be avoided, and manifold obligations to be discharged, as well as great happiness to be enjoyed. And should no provision be made? For lack of this, results in the frequent disappointments of that honorable estate. Hence that repentance which is at once too soon and too late. The husband does not know how to rule; and the wife does not know how to obey."*

> *"Women are not for rule designed,*
> *Nor yet for blind submission. Happy they*
> *Who, while they feel it pleasure to obey,*
> *Have yet a kind companion at their side,*
> *Who in the journey will his power divide,*
> *Or yield the reins, and bid the lady guide;*
> *Then points the wonders of the way, and makes*
> *The duty pleasant that she undertakes;*
> *He shows the objects as they pass along,*
> *And gently rules the movements that are wrong;*
> *He tells her all the skilful driver's art,*
> *And smiles to see how well she acts her part;*
> *Nor praise denies to courage or to skill,*
> *In using power, that he resumes at will."*

CHAPTER 2
The Family Circle

CHAPTER 2
The Family Circle

"Home!
There's magic in that little word;
It is a mystic circle which surrounds
Comforts and virtues, never known
Beyond the hallowed limit."

A family! How delightful are the associations we form
with such a word! How pleasing are the images with
which it crowds the mind and how tender are the
emotions that it awakens in the heart! Who can wonder
that domestic happiness should be a theme so dear
to poetry and that it should have called forth some
of the sweetest strains of fancy and feeling? Or who
can be surprised that of all the objects which present
themselves on the horizon of the future during this
journey of life, marriage should excite the most ardent
desires and engage the most active pursuits? But, alas,
of those who, in the ardor of youth, rush for the
possession of this dear prize, how many fail! And why?
Because their imagination alone is engaged upon the
subject and they have no definite idea of what it means
or of the way in which it is to be obtained. It is a mere

lovely dream of a romantic mind and oftentimes, with such persons, it fades away.

> *"And, like the baseless fabric of a vision,*
> *Leaves not a wreck behind."*

Therefore, it may be of service to consider the sources of domestic happiness and to show that they are to be found, not in the flowery regions of imagination, but in the sober realities of piety, chaste love, prudence, and well formed relationships. These precious springs of domestic happiness are within the reach of all who will take the path that leads to them, that is, the path of knowledge. We must make ourselves acquainted with the nature, the design, and the importance of the family compact. We must analyze this union to ascertain its various elements, its laws, and its purposes. Who can be a good citizen of any state without being acquainted with its constitution and the laws by which it is governed? It is equally vain to look for domestic happiness without clear insight and understanding of the purposes and the laws that Providence has laid down in the formation of a household.

Family Structure & Government

In the discussions that have been stirred up in order to settle the question as to which form of civil government is best adapted to secure the welfare of the human race, the family constitution has been too much overlooked. Speculation has been indulged and theories proposed by their respective authors, in reference to the greater aggregations of society, with all confidence and authority, while it is evident at the same time that they have forgotten how much the wellbeing of states is dependent on the wellbeing of the families of which *all* states are composed.

If there is any truth in the figure by which a nation is compared to a pillar, we should recollect that, while individuals are the materials of which the pillar is formed, it is the good condition of families that constitutes the cement and holds it together, giving solidity and durability to its form. If this is lacking, however inherently excellent the materials, however elegant the shape, however ornamental the base, the column, and the capital may be, it contains in itself a principle of decay, which is the active cause of dilapidation and ultimate ruin.

The domestic structure is a divine institute. God formed it himself. *He takes the solitary, and sets them in families.*[1] And, like the rest of God's works, this is done well and done wisely. It is, as a system of government, quite unique; neither below the heavens nor above them, is there anything precisely like it. In some respects, it resembles the civil government of a state and in others, the ecclesiastical rule of a church, and it is here that church and state may be said to meet. This meeting, however, is only on a very small scale and under very peculiar circumstances. When directed as it should be, every family has a sacred character, inasmuch as the head of it acts the part of both prophet and priest of the household, by instructing them in the knowledge of God and leading them in the worship of God while, at the same time, discharging the duties of a king by supporting a system of order, subordination, and discipline.

Conformable with its nature is its design. Beyond the benefit of the individuals who compose it and whose benefit is its first and immediate object, it is intended to promote the welfare of the national community to

1. Psalm 68:6.

which it belongs and of which it is a part. Hence, every nation has stamped a high value on the family compact, and guarded it with the most powerful sanctions. Well instructed, well ordered, and well governed families are the springs, which, from their depths, send forth the tributaries that by their confluence form the majestic flow of national greatness and prosperity. No state can be prosperous when family order and subordination is predominantly neglected, nor can any state be anything other than prosperous when family order and subordination is predominantly maintained.

It is certain that, under the wise instruction and the impartial rule of a father and within the little family circle, the son becomes a good citizen. It is by the fireside and upon the family hearth that loyalty and patriotism, and every public virtue is planted and grows. It is just as certain that it is from within disordered families that factious demagogues,[1] tumultuous rebels, and tyrannical oppressors are trained up to be their neighbors' torment or their country's plague.[2] It is there that the thorn and the brier, to use the elegant simile of the prophet, or the myrtle and the fir tree, are reared, which will in the future be the deformity and misery or the ornament and defense of the land.

But has the domestic structure a reference to only the present world and its perishable interests? By no means. All of God's arrangements for man reveal him[3] and are chiefly intended for him, in his relation to eternity, so that his eye is on that immortality to which he has

1. *factious demagogues*: insubordinate, dissension stirring leaders who acquire power by appealing to passions and prejudices.

2. *plague*: a scourge or disease that corrupts.

3. *reveal him*: that is, his arrangements and institutions reveal his sovereignty and attributes; e.g., God the Father, God the husband, God the lawgiver, God the provider, God the instructor, God the disciplinarian, God the comforter, etc.

destined the human race. The family has, in fact, a sacred character belonging to it, which may indeed be forgotten or disdained within some families, but the family itself is constituted and should, therefore, be conducted with the prospect in mind, of the upcoming generation following the one that precedes it not only to the grave, but to eternity.

Each Family Member, an Immortal Soul

Every member of every household is an immortal creature and every one that leaves the circle by death goes into an eternity of torment or bliss. Now, since all the institutes of God look to eternity as their chief and ultimate reference, surely, that institute which is the most powerful of all in the formation of character, must be considered as set up by God with a special intention to prepare the subjects of it for *"glory, honor, immortality, and eternal life."*[1]

When Faith is not a Family's Foundation

Where religion is missing as the basis of the marriage union, the happy fruits of it cannot be expected. How many interesting households are there to be found, in which all the social virtues are cultivated with assiduity, in which domestic charities flourish and public excellence is cherished, but in which they, on account of their lack of vital godliness, are still missing the highest end of their family union. They provide no preparatory course of education for heaven and eternity and so they are destined to be swept away with the wreck of the nations that did not know God and with the wicked who shall be cast into hell. Alas, that from such sweet scenes, such lovely retreats of connubial love

1. Romans 2:7.

and domestic peace, to which learning, science, wealth, and elegance have all been admitted, religion should be excluded! And while many wise and interesting guests are continually welcomed into the house, only Jesus Christ should be refused, who, wherever he goes, carries salvation in his train and makes those joys immortal which would otherwise soon perish forever.

Everlasting Bonds of a Believing Family

Precious, indeed, are the joys of a happy family—but, oh, how fleeting! How soon the circle must be broken up and how sudden it may be! What scenes of delight, resembling the happy visions of fairy tale bliss, have all been unexpectedly wrapped in shadow and gloom by misfortune, sickness, and death! The last enemy has entered the paradise and, by expelling one of its tenants, has embittered the scene to the rest. The ravages of death have been in some cases followed by the desolations of poverty and those, who once dwelt together in the happy enclosure of family, have been separated and scattered to meet no more. But religion, true religion, if it is possessed, will gather them together again after the destruction of all earthly ties and will conduct them to another paradise into which no calamity shall ever enter and from which no joy shall ever depart.[1]

Happy would it be, for all who stand related by family ties, if the bonds of nature were hallowed and rendered permanent by those of divine grace. To found our union on any other basis which does not contain religion in its formation is to erect it on quicksand and expose it to the fury of a thousand powerful waves, each of which

---

1. "God shall wipe away all tears from their eyes; and there shall be no more death, nor sorrow, nor crying; neither shall there be any more pain: for the former things are passed away." Revelation 21:4.

may overturn the fabric of our comfort in a moment. But to rest it upon religion is to found it upon a rock, where we shall each individually find a refuge even when the nearest and dearest relations are swept away by the tide of dissolution.

Independent & Flourishing Nature of the Domestic Constitution

It is a pleasing reflection that the domestic constitution does not depend upon either family possessions or the forms of national policy for its existence, its laws, its right administration, or its rich advantages. It may live and flourish in all its tender kindnesses, all its sweet pleasures, and all its moral power in the cottage as well as in the mansion, under the shadow of liberty or even under the scorching heat of tyranny. Like the church, of which it is in some respects the emblem, it accommodates itself to every changing form of surrounding society and to every nation and every age. Forming with the church the only two institutions ever set up by God, as to their framework, the family, like its kindred institute, remains amidst the ruins of the fall, the lapse of ages, and the changes of human affairs. It is the monument of what has been and the standing prediction of what will be.

Domestic Happiness, a Gift of God

Domestic happiness, in many ways, resembles the manna that was granted to the Israelites in the wilderness. Like that precious food, it is the gift of God, which comes down from heaven. It cannot be purchased with money, it is dispensed alike to the rich and the poor, and it accommodates itself to every taste. It is given with an abundance that meets the needs of all who desire it. To be obtained, it must be religiously sought in God's own way of bestowing it and it is granted to man as a refreshment during his pilgrimage through this wilderness to the celestial Canaan.

"*By you*
Founded in reason, loyal, just, and pure,
Relations dear, and all the charities
Of father, son, and brother first were known.
Far be it, that I should write you sin or blame,
Or think you unbefitting holiest place,
Perpetual fountain of domestic sweets!"

Milton

CHAPTER 3
Mutual Duties of a
Husband & Wife

CHAPTER 3
Mutual Duties of a Husband & Wife

"See that you love one another with a pure heart fervently." 1 Peter 1:22

Marriage is the foundation of the domestic structure. *"Marriage,"* says the apostle, *"is honorable among all."*[1] The same apostle has condemned the opinion of those by whose custom marriage is forbidden, showing that opinion, in fact, to be a *"doctrine of devils."*[2] Marriage was instituted by God, established in Eden, honored by the personal attendance of Christ at the wedding in Cana, and it even furnished an occasion for the first of that glorious series of miracles by which Christ manifested himself to be the Son of God and the Savior of the world.[3] Yet, there is another mark of distinction

1. "Marriage is honorable among all and the bed undefiled." Hebrews 13:4. The Greek is "he koite amiantos," the "bed," or literally the "sex," is "undefiled;" or, more obvious in the Latin Vulgate, "inmaculatus" or "immaculate."
2. "Some shall depart from the faith, giving heed to seducing spirits, and doctrines of devils, speaking lies in hypocrisy, having their conscience seared with a hot iron, forbidding to marry, and commanding to abstain from meats, which God has created to be received with thanksgiving by them that believe and know the truth." 1 Timothy 4:1-3.
3. Marriage is also held up to the highest degree of holy expectation in

that is placed upon marriage by the Holy Spirit, where it is said, *"This is a great mystery, but I speak concerning Christ and the church."*[1]

Many consider the term *"mystery"* as having no allusion to the nuptial tie, but as applying exclusively to the union of Christ and the church. If this is the case, it seems difficult to account for the introduction of this union at all, or to explain what bearing it has upon the subject at hand. Besides, the twofold reference to the mediatorial undertaking of Christ, which is made by the apostle when he enforces the duties of husband and wife, seems to confirm the opinion that he represents the conjugal union as a type or symbol of the close and endearing relation in which the church stands to its divine Redeemer. Nothing can throw a higher sanctity over the marital relationship, nor invest it with greater honor, than such a view of it.

Distinguishing, as it does, man from brute beasts; providing, not only for the continuance, but for the comfort of our species; containing in one the source of human happiness and of those virtuous emotions and generous sensibilities that adorn and refine the character of man, marriage can never, as a general subject, be guarded with too much solicitous vigilance, nor be formed, in particular instances, with too much prudence and care.

Love One Another Fervently

In proportion to the importance of the relationship itself, is an accurate view of and a due performance of the obligations arising out of it.

the Seventh and Tenth Commandments (Deuteronomy 5:18 and 21).
   1. Ephesians 5:32.

The first duty of marriage and the foundation of all other marital duties is love.[1] Let this be lacking and marriage is degraded at once into a brutal or a sordid compact.

> *"Love is a plant of holier birth*
> *Than any that takes root on earth;*
> *A flower from heaven, which it is a crime*
> *To number with the things of time."*

This duty, which is especially enjoined upon the husband, though for reasons we shall consider in another chapter, belongs equally to the wife. Love must be mutual or there can be no happiness. None for the party that does not love: for how dreadful is the idea of being chained for life to an individual for whom we have no affection and to be almost always in the company of a person from whom we are driven back by revulsion—yet driven back upon a bond that prevents separation and escape. Nor can there be any happiness for the party that does love, for, such an

---

1. "'*Love suffers long;*' is patient and forbearing under injuries and annoyances, and does not revile, revenge, or retaliate:—'*is kind;*' is not harsh or rude, but ever ready, willing, and pleased by looks, words, and actions, to promote the comfort of others:—'*does not envy;*' does not pine and grieve at the sight of another's superior possessions, fame, happiness, or piety, and dislike him on that account:—'*does not parade itself, is not puffed up;*' neither boasts of its own gifts, achievements, and possessions, nor despises others, nor makes insulting comparisons, but is humble and gentle ... '*does not seek its own;*' does not selfishly want to have its own way; to promote its own interest, to the neglect of others:—'*is not easily provoked;*' governs its temper, controls its passions, and is not soon or unreasonably irritable or petulant:—'*thinks no evil;*' is not censorious, nor forward to impute a bad motive to a doubtful action, but is disposed to put the best construction on actions and words:—'*does not rejoice in iniquity, but rejoices in the truth;*' does not delight in the sins, but in the excellences ... '*endures all things;*' bears hardships, sustains labor, makes sacrifices in order to accomplish its purposes of good-will. (1 Corinthians 4-7). Such is love in exercise and act. This is benevolence." John Angell James, Pastoral Addresses.

unrequited affection must either soon expire or live only to consume the miserable heart in which it burns.

Warning Beacon of Loveless Marriages

A married couple that lacks mutual affection is one of the most pitiable spectacles on earth. They cannot and, indeed, in ordinary circumstances, should not separate, and yet they remain united only to be a torment to one another. They serve one important purpose, however, in the history of mankind, and that is to be a beacon to all those who are yet single and to warn them against the sin and folly of forming a marriage union upon any other basis than that of a pure and mutual affection. They stand as a compelling admonition to all those who are already united, to guard their mutual affection with unceasing vigilance, so that nothing may be allowed to dampen that sacred flame.

Guarding & Preserving Affection

As the marriage union should be formed on the basis of love, so should great care be taken, especially in the early stages of it, that nothing might arise to unsettle or loosen our affections. Whatever knowledge we may obtain about each other's tastes and habits before marriage, it is never as accurate, as comprehensive, or as impressive upon us as the knowledge we acquire by living together. It is of the utmost consequence that when little defects are first noticed and trivial faults and oppositions first occur, they should not be allowed to produce an unfavorable impression upon our minds.

Man and wife are equally careful to avoid offending one another at the beginning of their relationship. Every little thing can wither a new blossom and every wind can shake loose a vine when it first begins to anchor itself. However, when by age and growth the vine is strong and securely anchored, and has brought forth its clusters, it can endure both storm and tempest and yet, never be broken. So are the beginnings of a marriage—watchful and observant, jealous and busy, inquisitive and careful, and apt to take alarm at every unkind word.

Faults and weaknesses do not manifest themselves in the first scenes, but in the course of a long companionship. And when faults appear at the first, it is not thought to be simple chance or weakness but rather it is feared to be a lack of love or prudence. That which appears ill at first usually affrights the inexperienced man or woman, who may jump to conclusions and imagine the worst, out of proportion to the new and early unkindness.

Plutarch compares a new marriage to a cask before the hoops are on it—that which it may and will hold, it cannot, but its tender structure being tested may fail. When the joints are strengthened however, and are bound firmly one to another, it can scarcely fail without fire or shattering violence. After the hearts of man and wife are endeared and confirmed in mutual confidence, through experience, and longer than artifice and pretence can last, there are many memories and things present that dash the little unkindnesses to pieces. For, it is either passion or folly, or a certain lack of love that cannot preserve the colors and beauties of kindness, so long as public honesty would require a man to wear his sorrow at every discontent.

Stifle Contention Before Quarrels Start

Let man and wife be careful to stifle little things, so that, as fast as they spring up, they are cut down and cast aside, for if these are allowed to remain and grow, they will make the atmosphere of the relationship irritable, the companionship troublesome, and the affections unstable and uneasy by habitual apprehension and ultimate aversion.[1]

Some people are more vexed by an annoying fly than they are by a wound. When gnats disturb the sleep and the reason is only half awakened, it is often seen that a person is more full of trouble than if when fully awake, they were to contend with a powerful enemy. In the frequent little accidents of family life, a person's reason cannot always be fully awake and, when they are troubled and a trifling matter makes them yet more troubled, weakness in them is soon betrayed in a storm of passion. It is certain that the man or woman is in a state of weakness and folly, when they can be troubled with a trifling accident. It is, therefore, not good to tempt their affections when they are in such a state.

In this case, be careful not to add fuel to the flame, for, that which is quickly kindled, is just as quickly extinguished, if it is not fanned or fed new materials. Do not add additional provocation to the incident and do not inflame it and peace will soon return and the incident and the discontent will pass away, like stray sparks that come to nothing. Always remember that discontents proceeding from little daily things, may breed a secret and indiscernible disease, which is more destructive than those sudden outbursts of weakness that are so easily extinguished.

Study One Another's Likes & Dislikes

If a couple would preserve love, let them be sure to accurately study each other's tastes and distastes and anxiously avoid that which they know to be contrary to

---

1. "The beginning of strife is like letting out water; therefore leave off contention, before there is quarreling." Proverbs 17:14.

them, even in the smallest things. The ancients, in their conjugal allegories, used to represent Mercury standing by Venus, to signify that by fair language and sweet entreaties, the minds of each other should be united.

Dangerous Distinctions of Mine & Yours

If a couple would preserve love, let them very carefully avoid all curious and frequently repeated distinctions of "mine" and "yours." For, such distinctions have brought about all the laws, all the lawsuits, and all the wars in the world. Let those, who are but *"one flesh,"* have but one interest. Instances may occur in which there may and must be a separate investiture of property and a sovereign and independent right of disposal in the woman. In this case, the husband should take the most anxious care not to attempt to invade her right, and the wife should take the most anxious care to neither ostentatiously speak of it, nor to rigidly claim it, nor to selfishly exercise it.

In ordinary cases, they should be heirs to each other if they die childless. And if there are children, the wife should be a partner with them in the inheritance. But during their life, the use and employment of goods must be common to both their necessities and in this there is no other difference of right, but that the man has the dispensation of all, as he who must properly balance all.

Mutual Respect & Respectability

Mutual respect is a duty of married life, and, although special reverence is due from the wife, as we will consider in a later chapter, yet respect is due from the husband also. As it is difficult to respect those who are not entitled to it on any other ground than superior rank or common relationship, it is of immense consequence that we act towards one another in a manner which deserves respect and commands it by its very merit.

Moral esteem is one of the strongest pillars and the most powerful safeguards of love. A high degree of moral excellence cannot fail to produce such esteem. We are more accurately known by each other in the marital relationship than we are by the world or even by our own children, coworkers, and employees. The privacy of such a relationship lays open our motives and all the interior of our character, so that we are sometimes better known to each other than we are to ourselves. Therefore, if we want to be respected, we must be respectable.

Love covers a multitude of faults,[1] it is true, but we must not presume too far upon the credulity and blindness of affection. There is a point beyond which even love cannot be blind to the crimson color of a guilty action. Every bit of real sinful conduct, the indecency of which cannot be mistaken, tends to sink the offender in the other's esteem. Perhaps this has not been sufficiently thought of in wedded life, the parties being sometimes anxious only to hide their delinquencies from the world, forgetful that it is a dreadful thing to lose one another's respect. It is delightfully striking to observe how some couples of eminent morality, regard each other—what reverence is blended with their love, what admiration, and how angelic in excellence do they appear to one another.

In all our conduct in the conjugal state, then, there should be the most obvious and unwavering mutual respect, even in little things. There must be no searching after faults, no examining with microscopic scrutiny

1. 1 Peter 4:8.

such faults as cannot be concealed, no reproachful nicknaming, no rude contempt, no incivility, and no cold neglect. There should be courtesy without ceremony, politeness without formality, and attentiveness without slavery. In short, there should be tender love supported by esteem and guided by politeness.

Likewise, then, we must maintain our mutual respectability before others. Strangers, friends, employees, coworkers, and children must all be taught to respect us by what they see in our own behavior. It is highly improper for either party to commit some act, to say any word, or assume any look, that will have the remotest tendency to lower the other in public esteem.

Mutual Companionship

Mutual attachment to each other's company is a common duty of husband and wife. We are united to be mutual companions: to live together, to walk together, and to talk together. The husband is commanded *to dwell with the wife according to knowledge.*[1] By "dwelling," says Mr. Jay, is intended nothing less than residence, as opposed to absence and roaming. It is absurd, for those who have no prospect of dwelling together, to enter into marriage and, for those who are already married, to be unnecessarily apart. Various circumstances will, of course, render occasional excursions from home unavoidable, but let a man return as soon as the purpose for his absence is accomplished. And, let him travel with the words of Solomon in his mind, *"As a bird that wanders from its nest, so is a man that wanders from his place."*[2] Can a man discharge the duties he owes to his household while he is away from home? Can he

1. 1 Peter 3:7. 2. Proverbs 27:8.

discipline his children? Can he oversee and ensure the worship of God in his family?

I know it is the duty of the wife to lead worship and Bible study in the absence of her husband. She must take it up as a duty, if not, during that time, as a privilege. For those, however, who are not so disposed, one of the sanctuaries of God is closed up for weeks and even months at a time.

I am sorry to say that there are some husbands who seem fonder of any other company than that of their wives. This plainly appears in how they spend their leisure hours; appropriating so few of them to the wife! The evenings are the most domestic periods of the day. The wife is peculiarly entitled to these evening hours. She is then most free from her numerous cares and most at liberty to enjoy reading and conversation. It is a sad reflection upon a man when he is fond of spending his evenings away from home. It implies something bad and it predicts something worse.

To ensure, as far as possible, the company of her husband at his own fireside, let the wife be a *keeper at home*[1] and do all that is in her power to render that home as attractive as a good temperament, neatness, and cheerful, affectionate conversation can make it. Let her strive to make his own home the cozy surrounding in which his heart might relax in the warmth of domestic enjoyment.

We can easily imagine that even in Paradise, when man had no guilt haunting him, no visions of crime, and no voice from a troubled conscience to disturb his peace, that even then, Adam did not like to find Eve absent from their home when he returned from the

---

1. Titus 2:5.

labor of dressing the garden. He wanted the smile of her countenance to light up his own and the music of her voice to be the melody of his soul. Think, then, how much more in his fallen state, with guilt upon his conscience and cares pressing down upon his heart, does a man now need, upon coming home from the scenes of his anxious toil, the aid of woman's companionship to drive away the cares that disquiet his heart; to smooth his furrowed brow; to tranquilize his agitated heart; and at once to both reprove and comfort his mind that has in some measure yielded to temptation.

Oh woman! You know the hour when he will return home, when the burdens of the day are past. Do not let him, at such a time, find upon his coming home to his habitation that the foot, which should run to meet him, is wandering at a distance. Let him enter a garden, a home set in order, where neatness delights and attracts. If the opposite is the case, who can wonder that in the anguish of disappointment and the bitterness of neglect, a husband turns away from his own door and looks in the houses of others for a substitute for both that comfort which he wished to enjoy at home and that companionship which he hoped to find in his wife?

Man and wife are united to be associates, therefore, let each be as much in the other's company as possible. I thank God, I am a stranger to that taste that leads a man to flee from his own comfortable living room and the society of his wife, from the instruction and recreation contained in a well stocked library, or from the evening rural walk, when the business of the day is over, to scenes of public entertainment for enjoyment. In my judgment, the pleasures of home and of home society, when they are all that could be desired, are such as can never be too much or in need of change, but satisfy from one kindred scene to another. I sigh and long, perhaps in vain, for a period when society might be elevated and purified, when the love of knowledge will be intense, and the habits of life so simple, and when true religion and morality will be so well diffused that men's homes will be the seat and circle of their pleasures. A time when, in the company of an affectionate and intelligent wife and well-disciplined children, each man will find his greatest earthly delight. When it will no longer be felt necessary for their happiness to leave their own homes for the theaters, pubs, and other public entertainments or to go from the well spread table at home to the public banquets, to satisfy the cravings of a healthy appetite. Then it will no longer be imposed upon preachers to show that the constant frequenting of public amusements is improper, for they will already be found unnecessary.

Public & Religious Duties

The pleasures of home, however, must not be allowed to interfere with the calls and claims of public duty. Wives must not ask and husbands must not give that time which is demanded for the cause of God and man. This is an age of active charity and the great public institutions that have been set up cannot be kept in operation without great sacrifices of time by very many persons. Those who, by their wisdom, talents, rank, or property, receive the confidence of the public, must be prepared to occupy and manage the executive departments of our charitable societies. They should not allow the soft allurements of their own homes to draw them away from what is also a post of duty.

We have known some, who, until they entered into wedded life, were the props and pillars of these institutions. They yield so far to the solicitations of their new and dearest earthly friend that they have vacated their seats on the board of management forever after. It is, I admit, a costly way of contributing to the cause of religion and humanity, to give those evening hours which could be spent so pleasantly in a country walk or in the joint perusal of some interesting volume, but who can do good or should wish to do good without some sacrifices? I know an eminently holy and useful minister, who told the lady to whom he was about to be united, that one of the conditions of their marriage was that she should never ask him for that time, which, on any occasion, he felt it to be his duty to give to God. And surely, any woman might feel herself more blessed in having to sometimes endure the loss of a husband's company, whose presence and talents are coveted by all public institutions, than in being left to the unmolested enjoyment of the company of one whose assistance is coveted by none.

Mutual Forbearance

Mutual forbearance is another duty.[1] This we owe to everyone,[2] not excluding the stranger or even an enemy[3] and, therefore, it certainly must not be denied to our nearest friend. For the love that *suffers long and is kind; that does not envy; does not vaunt itself, is not puffed*

---

1. "Be kind to one another, tenderhearted, forgiving one another, even as God for Christ sake has forgiven you." Ephesians 4:32. "Put on therefore, as the elect of God, holy and beloved, bowels of mercies, kindness, humbleness of mind, meekness, longsuffering; forbearing one another, and forgiving one another, if any man has a quarrel against any; even as Christ forgave you, so also you do." Colossians 3:12-13.

2. "For if you forgive men their trespasses, your heavenly Father will also forgive you: but if you do not forgive men their trespasses, neither will your Father forgive your trespasses." Matthew 6:14-15.

3. "Love your enemies, bless them that curse you, do good to them that hate you, and pray for them that spitefully use you, and persecute you; that you may be the children of your Father who is in heaven: for he makes his sun rise on the evil and on the good." Matthew 5:44-45.

up; that does not behave unseemly; does not seek its own, is not easily provoked, thinks no evil; does not rejoice in iniquity, but rejoices in the truth; bears all things, believes all things, hopes all things, endures all things,"[1] for this love there is both need and room in every relationship. Wherever sin or imperfection exists, there is scope for the forbearance of love. There is no perfection upon earth. Lovers, it is true, often fancy they have found it, but the more sober judgment of husbands and wives generally corrects the mistake. First impressions of this kind usually pass away with first love.

We should all enter the state of marriage remembering that we are about to be united to a fallen creature. In every case, as it is not two angels that have met together, but two sinful children of Adam, from whom much weakness and waywardness must be expected, we must resign ourselves to some imperfection.[2] Remembering that we have no small share of our own faults that call for the forbearance of the other party, we ourselves should exercise the very patience that we ask of them.[3] As both husband and wife have sinful frailties and as they are so constantly together, innumerable occasions will be furnished for contention if they are eager or even a little willing to avail themselves to such opportunities.[4] Those occasions, if they do not produce a chilling effect on our love, will at least lead to an interruption of it, however temporary. Many things we should connive at,

---

1. 1 Corinthians 13:4-7.

2. "For there is not a just man on earth that does good and does not sin." Ecclesiastes 7:20.

3. "Whatsoever you would that men should do to you, even so do you to them: for this is the law and the prophets." Matthew 7:12. "Also do not take to heart every word that is spoken, lest you hear your servant curse you. For oftentimes, also, your own heart knows that you yourself have cursed others." Ecclesiastes 7:21-22.

4. "The beginning of strife is like letting out water; therefore leave off contention, before there is quarreling." Proverbs 17:14.

others we should pass by with an unprovoked mind, and in all things, most carefully avoid even what at first may seem to be an innocent disputation.

Mutual Correction & Reproof

Affection does not forbid, but actually demands that we point out one another's faults.[1] Yet, this should be done in all the meekness of wisdom,[2] united with all the tenderness of love,[3] lest we only increase our troubles. Justice, as well as wisdom, requires that, in every case, we set the good qualities against the bad ones. In most cases, we shall find some redeeming excellences, which, if they cannot reconcile us to the failings we deplore, should at least teach us to bear them with patience. The more we contemplate these better aspects of each other's character, the brighter they will appear, for it is an undeniable fact that, while faults diminish, virtues magnify in proportion as they are steadily contemplated.

As to bitterness of language and violence of conduct,[4] this is so utterly disgraceful that it scarcely needs to be discussed, even by way of cautioning against it. We are told that the ancients took the gall from their nuptial sacrifices and cast it behind the altar to intimate the removal of all bitterness from the marriage state.

1. "You shall not hate your brother in your heart. You shall surely rebuke your neighbor, and not suffer sin upon him." Leviticus 19:17.
2. James 3:13.
3. "If a man is overtaken in any trespass, you who are spiritual, restore such a one in a spirit of meekness; considering yourself, lest you also be tempted. Bear one another's burdens, and so fulfill the law of Christ." Galatians 6:1-2.
4. "The Lord tries the righteous: but the wicked and him that loves violence his soul hates." Psalm 11:5.

Mutual Help & Assistance

Mutual assistance is the duty of husbands and wives.[1] This applies to all the cares of life. Even when a woman is not very conversant in matters of trade, her counsel may still be sought with propriety and advantage in a thousand cases. The husband should never undertake anything of importance without communicating the matter to his wife. Likewise, she should invite him to communicate freely all his anxieties, instead of shrinking from the responsibility of a counselor and leaving him to struggle alone with the difficulties and perplexities that he faces. For, if she cannot counsel, she can comfort; if she cannot relieve his cares, she can help to bear them; if she cannot direct the course of his trade, she may the current of his feelings; if she cannot open any source of earthly wisdom, she can spread the matter before the Father and Fountain of lights. Many men, under the idea of delicacy to their wives, keep all their difficulties to themselves, which only leaves them without comfort, counsel, and advice, and leaves them to bear a blow the heavier if it does come.

Likewise, then, just as the wife should be willing to help her husband in matters of business, he should be willing to share her burden of domestic anxieties and fatigue. Some go too far, however, and utterly degrade the female head of the family by treating her as if her honesty or ability cannot be trusted in the management of the household economy. They keep the money and dole it out as if they were parting with their life's blood, grudging every penny they dispense and

1. "Matrimony or wedlock is a state or a degree ordained by God and an office wherein the husband serves the wife and the wife the husband. It was ordained for a remedy and to increase the world, and for the man to help the woman and the woman to help the man with all love and kindness." William Tyndale, The Obedience of a Christian Man (1528).

requiring an account of it as rigidly as they would from a suspected servant. They take charge of everything, give out everything, and interfere in everything. This is to rob a woman of her authority, to thrust her from her proper place, and to insult and degrade her before her children and others.

Some, on the other hand, go to the opposite extreme and take no share in anything. My heart has ached to see the slavery of some devoted, hardworking, and ill-used wives. After laboring all day amidst the ceaseless toils of a family, they have had to pass the evening hours in solitude while their husbands, instead of coming home to cheer them with their companionship or to relieve them for even half an hour of their fatigue, have occupied themselves with some other entertainment or have gone out with their friends or even to a sermon. Then these unfortunate women have had to stay awake and watch all night long over a sick or restless child, while the men, whom they accepted as the partners of their sorrows, slept soundly, unwilling to give up even a single hour of their slumber, although it would have allowed a little repose to their toil worn wives.

Even irrational creatures shame such men, for, it is a well known fact that the male bird takes his turn on the nest during the season of incubation, to allow the female time to renew her strength with food and rest. He also goes with her in the diligent quest for food and feeds the young ones when they cry. No man should think of marrying, who does not stand prepared to share with his wife the burden of domestic cares, as far as he can do it.

Mutual Assistance in Personal Religion

Man and wife should be helpful to one another in the concerns of personal religion. This duty is clearly implied in the apostle's language: *"For what do you know, oh wife, whether you shall save your husband? Or how do you know, oh man, whether you shall save your wife?"*[1] Where only one is yet a partaker of true piety, there should be the most anxious, judicious, and affectionate efforts for the other's salvation. Where both parties are real Christians, there should be the exercise of a constant reciprocal solicitude, watchfulness, and care, with respect to their spiritual and eternal welfare.

> *"How blest the sacred tie that binds*
> *In union sweet accordant minds!*
> *How swift the heavenly course they run,*
> *Whose hearts, whose faith, whose hopes are one!"*

One of the ends which every believer must propose to himself, on entering the state of marriage, is to secure a faithful friend who will be a helpmate to him in reference to the world to come, assist him in the great business of his soul's salvation, and pray for him and with him. One that will affectionately tell him of his sins and defects, viewed in the light of a Christian. One that will stimulate and draw him by the power of a holy example and the sweet force of persuasive words. One that will warn him in temptation, comfort him in dejection, and in every way assist him in his pilgrimage to heaven.

The highest purpose of the connubial state is lost, if it is not rendered helpful to our piety, and yet this end is all too commonly neglected, even by those who profess religion. Do we converse with each other as we should on the subjects of redemption through Jesus Christ and of eternal salvation? Do we study one another's dispositions, the snares and troubles we are each subject

1. 1 Corinthians 7:16.

to, and the erosions of one another's piety brought on by the influences of this world, that we may apply suitable remedies? Do we *exhort one another daily, lest we should be hardened through the deceitfulness of sin?*[1] Do we practice fidelity without censoriousness, and administer praise without flattery? Do we invite one another to the most quickening and edifying public means of grace and recommend the perusal of such instructive and improving books as we have found beneficial to ourselves? Do we mutually lay open the state of our minds on the subject of personal religion and state our perplexities, our joys, our fears, our sorrows? Alas, alas, who must not blush at their neglect in these particulars? Yet such neglect is as criminal as it is common. Fleeing from the wrath to come and yet not doing all that we can to aid each other's escape! Contending side by side for the crown of *glory, honor, immortality, and eternal life,*[2] and yet not doing all that we can to ensure each other's success! Is this love? Is this the tenderness of connubial affection?

This mutual help should extend to the maintenance of all the habits of domestic order, discipline, and piety. The husband is to be the instructor, intercessor, and governor of the family:[3] to guide their minds in godliness and truth, to lead their devotions, and to govern their tempers. And in all that relates to these important objects, the wife is to be of one mind with him. They are, in these matters, to be workers together,

---

1. Hebrews 3:13.   2. Romans 2:7.

3. As head of the household, the husband is primarily responsible for the spiritual governing and nurturing of his family. He is to emulate Christ's active care over the church in his own active care over his household—striving for their purity. He must lead them both by fervent instruction in the Word of God and by a gentle and godly example, in all things. Just as Joshua said, "As for me and my house, we will serve the Lord" (Joshua 21:15), so he must say and so he must do.

neither of them leaving the other to labor alone, much less opposing or thwarting what is done. *"When the sun shines, the moon disappears; when he sets, she appears and shines; so when the husband is at home, he leads domestic worship, when he is absent, the wife must ever take his place."*

Some men refer the instruction of their young children exclusively to their wives and some wives, as soon as the children are too old to be taught upon the knee, think that they are exclusively the subjects of fatherly care. This is a mistake in the all important economy of the family, the members of which are never too young to be taught and disciplined by the father, nor too old to be admonished and warned by the mother. He may sometimes have a great influence in awing the unruly spirits of the younger children, while her soft, persuasive words may have delightful power in melting or breaking the hard and stubborn hearts of the older ones. Thus, they who have a joint interest in the family, must attend to them in a joint exercise of the labor.

Mutual Assistance in Humane & Religious Charity

Husband and wife must be helpful to one another in works of humane and religious charity. Their mutual influence should be exerted, not in restraining, but in stimulating zeal, compassion, and liberality. What a beautiful portrait of domestic life was drawn by the pen of the Old Testament writer: *"It fell on a day, that Elisha passed to Shunem, where there was a great woman, and she constrained him to eat bread. And so it was, that as often as he passed by, he turned in there to eat bread. And she said to her husband, Behold now, I perceive that this is a holy man of God, which passes by us continually. Let us make a little chamber on the wall, and let us set a bed for him there, and a table, and a stool, and a candlestick, and it shall be, that when he comes to us, he can turn in there. And it fell on a day that he came there, and he turned into the chamber, and lay there.*[1]

Every part of this scene is lovely: the generous and pious wish of the wife to provide accommodation for a prophet; her prompt and prudent effort to interest her husband in her kindhearted scheme; her discretion and modesty in keeping her place as a wife, by not acting without his permission; and her dignified claim of a right to be associated with him in this work of mercy, for, she said, "let *us* make a little chamber on the wall." All of this story is delightful and it exemplifies just how things should be on the part of a wife and no less so on the part of a husband. For, he gave no rude refusal or proud rejection of her plan because it did not originate from him, nor did he offer any covetous plea to set it aside on the grounds of expense.

Delighted to gratify the benevolent wishes and to support the liberal schemes of his wife, as every husband should be as far as prudence will allow, he consented. The little room was erected and furnished by this holy couple and the prophet soon occupied it. Never was a generous action more speedily or more richly rewarded. Elisha had no means of his own by which to acknowledge the kindness, but he who said in after times, *"He that receives a prophet in the name of a prophet shall receive a prophet's reward,"*[2] took upon himself, as he does in every instance, the cause of his necessitous servant and most munificently repaid the generous deed.

A lovelier scene cannot be found upon earth, than that of a pious couple employing their mutual influence

---

1. 2 Kings 4:8-11.   2. Matthew 10:41.

and personal leisure hours, in stirring up one another's hearts to deeds of mercy and religious compassion. Not even Adam and Eve in Paradise, with the unspotted robes of their innocence upon them, engaged in tending the vines or trailing the roses of the garden, could have presented a more interesting spectacle to the eyes of angels. What a contrast does such a godly pair present in comparison to other couples. The godly concern themselves with what they can save from unnecessary expenses that they might bestow it upon the cause of God and humanity, while others withhold from the claims of charity, to spend it upon fine furniture or domestic luxuries.

Are there not wives who attempt to chill the ardor, limit the beneficence, and curb the charitableness of their husbands? Who, by quarrelsome suggestions insinuate that he is doing too much for others and not enough for his own family,[1] driving the good man to exercise his liberality in secret and bestow his charities by stealth, even though he is lord of his own property? And what is frequently the objective of such women? Nothing more than the pride of ambition or the folly of vanity that they might have these parings of charity, to spend on clothing, furniture, and parties.

Perhaps the question will be asked, whether it is proper for a wife to give away the money earned by her husband in acts of humanity or religious benevolence. Such an inquiry should not be necessary, for no woman should be driven to the choice of either doing nothing

---

1. "Not, however, that [charity] overlooks the ties of social existence, and with infidel licentiousness merges the regard which is due to individual relationships, in the wild notion of a universal philanthropy: no: it *begins* with these, and is founded upon them (1 Timothy 5:8), though it stops not in them, but goes out and on, to all beyond this comparatively narrow circle." John Angell James, Pastoral Addresses.

for the cause of God and man or doing only what she can by stealth. A sufficient sum should be placed at her disposal to enable her to enjoy the luxury of doing good. Why should she not appear in her own name on the honorable list of benefactors and shine forth in her peculiar and separate glory, instead of being always lost in the radiance of her husband's record of mercy? Why should she have no sphere of benevolent effort and why should we monopolize to ourselves the blessings of those that are ready to perish?

It is the degrading of a married woman to allow her no discretion in this matter, no liberty of distribution, no power to dispense, but to compel her to beg first from her husband that which others come to beg of her. If, however, she is unhappily united to a Nabal,[1] a churl, whose sordid, grasping, covetous disposition will yield nothing to the claims of humanity or true religion, the question may be asked whether she might make up for the deficiency of her husband and diffuse any property unknown to him? I am strongly tempted to answer this question in the affirmative, for, if there were ever an instance where we might take a man at his word and act upon it, perhaps this is such a case. It was he who said, in the solemn act of matrimony, "with all my worldly goods I endow you," investing the wife with joint proprietorship and the right of appropriation.

But, we must not sacrifice the general principles by which we live to special cases as that found in the story of Nabal. I, therefore, say to every woman in such circumstances, obtain, if you can, a separate and fixed allowance for charitable distribution, but if even this is not possible, obtain one for general personal expenses and by a most rigid frugality save what you can from

1. 1 Samuel 25:2-42.

dress and decoration, for the hallowed purpose of relieving the miseries of others.

Mutual Sympathy & Care

Sickness may call for mutual sympathy and women seem to be both formed and inclined by nature to yield it.

> *"Oh woman, in our hours of ease,*
> *Uncertain, coy, and hard to please,*
> *And variable as the shade*
> *By the light, quivering aspen made,*
> *When pain and anguish wring the brow,*
> *A ministering angel thou!"*

Unwilling and, indeed, unable to subscribe to the former part of this description, I do most readily assent to the truth of the latter. Even if we could do without her and be happy in health, what are we in sickness without her presence and her tender care? Can we smooth the pillow or administer the medicine and the food as she can? No. There is a softness in her touch, a lightness in her step, a skill in her arrangements, and an unmistakable sympathy looking down upon us from her eyes. Many a woman, by her devoted and kind attentions in a season of sickness, has drawn back to herself that cold and alienated heart, which neither her charms could hold nor her claims recover.

I entreat you married women, therefore, to put forth all your power to soothe and please in the season of your husband's sickness. Let him see you willing to make those sacrifices of your pleasure, comfort, and sleep to minister to his comfort. Let there be a tenderness in your manner, a wakeful attention and sympathy in your look, a something that seems to say that your only comfort in his affliction is to employ yourself in alleviating it. Listen with patience and kindness to the tale of his lighter and even imaginary woes. A cold, heartless, awkward, and unsympathetic woman is the exception from the general rule, and how much more so, then, from the Christian.

This sympathy is not exclusively the duty of the wife, but belongs equally to the husband. He cannot, it is true, perform the same offices for her that she is able to discharge for him, but he can do much for her comfort, and all he can do he should do. Her sicknesses are generally more numerous and heavy than his and she is likely, therefore, to make more frequent calls upon his tender interest and attention. Many of her ailments are the consequence of becoming his wife. She was, perhaps, in full vitality until she became a mother, and from that time never had a moment's perfect ease or strength again. That event, which sent into his heart the joys of parenthood, may have dismissed from her frame the comforts of health. And shall he look with discontent and indifference, and insensibility, upon the women, who, before he transplanted her into his home as a wife and mother, glowed with beauty, to the admiration of every spectator? Shall he now cease to regard her with any pleasure, or sympathy, and seem as if he wished her gone to make room for another, forgetting that it was he that brought upon her the changes of motherhood and the imperfections of health and body?

Husbands, I call upon you for all the skill and tenderness of love, on behalf of your wives, if they are of a weak or sickly constitution. Watch by their bed, talk with them, and pray with them. In all their afflictions, you also be afflicted. Never listen heedlessly to their complaints and, by all that is sacred in conjugal affection, I implore you to never, by your cold neglect or petulant expressions, or discontented look, to call up in their imaginations, which may be unusually sensitive at such a time, even the remotest fear that the disease, which has destroyed their health, has done the same to your affections. Oh, spare her heart the agonizing pangs of thinking that she has become a burden and a disappointment to you.

The cruelty of that man wants a name and I know of none sufficiently emphatic, who denies his sympathy to a suffering woman, whose only failure is a broken constitution and whose calamity is the result of her marriage. Such a man does the work of one who destroys a life, without his punishment and, in some instances, without his reproach.

Sympathy should be exercised by man and wife toward one another not only in sickness, but in all afflictions. All their sorrows should be common.[1] Like two strings in unison, the chord of grief should never be struck in the heart of one without causing a corresponding vibration in the heart of the other. Like the surface of the lake answering to the heaven, it should be impossible for calmness and sunshine to be upon one while the other is agitated and cloudy. Heart should answer to heart, and face to face.

---

1. For, so we are commanded in the Gospel: "Rejoice with them that rejoice, and weep with them that weep." Romans 12:15.

CHAPTER 4
Special Duties of a Husband

CHAPTER 4
Special Duties of a Husband

"Husbands, love your wives, even as Christ also loved the church, and gave himself for it." Ephesians 5:25

In stating the duties especially enjoined upon the two parties in the conjugal union, I shall begin with those of the husband. He is commanded to *love*[1] his wife.

Husbands Love Your Wives

As we have already shown that love is a duty of both parties, the question very naturally arises, "For what reason is it so especially enjoined upon the husband?" Why is he so particularly bound to the exercise of affection? Perhaps it is for the following reasons:

1. Because, in the very nature of things, he is the most in danger of failing in his duty. Placed by the Creator

---

1. "The love of the husband is counseling and comforting, providing and protecting." William Bates, Spiritual Perfection Unfolded and Enforced.

"Love suffers long and is kind; love does not envy; love does not vaunt itself, is not puffed up; does not behave unseemly, does not seek its own, is not provoked, thinks no evil; does not rejoice in iniquity, but rejoices in the truth; bears all things, believes all things, hopes all things, endures all things. Love never fails." 1 Corinthians 13:4-8.

as the *"head of the wife"*[1] and invested with a certain right to govern his household, he is more in peril of setting aside the tender sensibilities for a predominant consciousness of superiority.

2. Because he is actually more deficient in this duty than the other party is. This has ever been the case in pagan and Mahometan countries. In barbarous nations, especially, conjugal affection has ever been exceedingly weak and it is probable that even in the more civilized countries of Greece and Rome it was not so generally strong and steady as Christianity has since made it. But without even going beyond the limits of Christendom, it may truly be said, that husbands are usually more deficient in love than wives. Wives, in my opinion, excel husbands in tenderness, strength, and constancy of affection.

3. Because a lack of love on the part of the man is likely to be attended with more misery to the other party. He can go to greater excesses in violence, cruelty, and depravity. The lack of this tender passion in him is likely to have a still worse effect upon his own character and upon the peace of the wife, than the lack of it in her. In either case, to be destitute of love is a melancholy thing, but in a husband it is, on several accounts, the more to be dreaded.

The apostle lays down two models or rules for a husband's affection: one is the love which Christ manifested for his church,[2] and the other is the love which a man bears for himself.[3]

---

1. "Wives, submit yourselves to your own husbands, as to the Lord. For the husband is head of the wife, even as Christ is head of the church: and he is the Savior of the body. Therefore, as the church is subject to Christ, so let the wives be to their own husbands in everything." Ephesians 5:22-24.

2. "As Christ also loved the church and gave himself for it." Ephesians 5:25.

3. "So ought husbands to love their wives as their own bodies; he that

As Christ Loved the Church

In regard to the first, I shall exhibit the properties of Christ's love and show in what way our affection should be conformed to his.

Christ's Love was Sincere

Christ's love was sincere. He did not *love in word only, but in deed and in truth.*[1] In him there was no dissimulation, no epithets of endearment spoken by feigned lips, and no actions varnished over with a mere covering of love. We must be like Christ and endeavor to maintain a principle of true regard in our heart as well as show true regard in our conduct. It is a miserable thing to have to act the part of love without feeling it. Hypocrisy in anything is base, but next to religion, hypocrisy is most base in affection. How difficult it is to act the part well, to keep on the mask, and to support the character so as to escape detection! Oh, the misery of that woman's heart, who at length finds out, to her own cost, that what she had been accustomed to receive and value as the attentions of a lover, are but the tricks of a cunning dissembler!

Christ's Love was Ardent

The love of the Redeemer was ardent. Let us, if we would form a correct idea of what should be the state of our hearts towards the woman of our choice, think of the affection that glowed in the breast of the Savior when he lived and died for his people. It is true, we can posses neither the same kind nor the same degree of

loves his wife loves himself. For no one ever hated his own flesh, but nourishes and cherishes it, even as the Lord does the church." Ephesians 5:28-29.

1. 1 John 3:18.

regard but, surely, when such an example is enjoined upon us, if not altogether as a model, yet as a motive, it teaches us that no weak affection is due or should be offered to the wife of our bosom. We are told by the Savior himself that if he laid down his life for us, it is our duty to lay down ours for the brethren. How much more for the *"friend that sticks closer than a brother!"*[1] And if it is our duty to lay down our life, how much more to employ it, while it lasts, in all the offices of a strong, steady, and creative affection. She, who for our sake has forsaken the comfortable home, watchful care, and warm embrace of her parents, has a right to expect from our affection that which will make her *"forget her father's house"* and cause her to feel that with respect to happiness she is no loser by the exchange. Happy the woman—and such should every husband strive to make his wife, who can look back without a sigh upon the moment when she left forever the guardians, companions, and scenes of her childhood!

Christ's Love was Supreme

The love of Christ to his church was supreme. He gives to the world his benevolence, but to the church his satisfaction. *"The Lord your God in the midst of you,"* said the prophet, *"is mighty; he will save; he will rejoice over you with joy; he will rest in his love; he will joy over you with singing."*[2] So must the husband regard his wife above all else: he must *"rest in his love."* He should regard her not only above all that is outside his house, but above all that is within it. She must take precedence, both in his heart and conduct, not only over all strangers but over all relatives[3] and also over all

---

1. Proverbs 18:24.   2. Zephaniah 3:17.
3. "A man shall leave his father and his mother and shall cleave to his wife, and they shall be one flesh." Genesis 2:24.

his children. He should love his children for her sake, rather than her for theirs. Is this already always the case? On the contrary, have we not often seen men who appear to be far more interested in their children than in their wives and who have paid far less attention to the latter than to grownup daughters? How especially unseemly is it for a man to be seen fonder of the company of any other woman than that of his wife, even where nothing more is intended than the pleasure of her company. Nor should he forsake her in his leisure hours for any companions of his own sex, no matter how interesting their personalities or conversation may be.

Christ's Love is Consistent

The love of Christ is consistent. Like him, it is *the same yesterday, today, and forever.*[1] Conjugal affection should have this same character. It should be alike at all times and in all places—the same at home as it is away from home, the same in other peoples' houses as it is in our own. Does many a wife not have to sigh and exclaim, "Oh that I were treated in my own home with the same tenderness and attention as I receive in company." With what loathing and revulsion must such a woman turn from endearments, which under such circumstances she can consider as nothing but hypocrisy. Home is the chief place for fond and minute attention and she, who does not have to complain of a lack of it there, will seldom feel the need or the inclination to complain of a lack of it away from the home, with the exception of those foolish women who would degrade their husbands by exacting not only what is truly kind, but what is actually ridiculous.

1. Hebrews 13:8.

Christ's Love was Providing

The love of the Redeemer was practical and laborious.[1] He provided everything by his mediation for the welfare and comfort of his church and at a cost and by exertions of which we can form no idea. It has been already declared that both parties are to assist in the cares of life. A good wife cannot be an idle one. Beautiful is that portrait of her drawn by the wise man:

> *"Who can find a virtuous woman? For her price is far above rubies. The heart of her husband safely trusts in her, so that he shall have no need of spoil. She will do him good and not evil all the days of her life. ... She lays her hands to the spindle, and her hands hold the distaff. She stretches out her hand to the poor; yes, she reaches out her hands to the needy. ... Her husband is known in the gates, when he sits among the elders of the land. ... She opens her mouth with wisdom, and in her tongue is the law of kindness. She looks well to the ways of her household, and does not eat the bread of idleness. Her children rise up and call her blessed; her husband also, and he praises her. Many daughters have done virtuously, but you excel them all. Favor is deceitful, and beauty is vain; but a woman that fears the Lord, she shall be praised. Give her the fruit of her hands, and let her own works praise her in the gates."*[2]

This exquisite picture, combining industry, prudence, dignity, meekness, wisdom, and piety cannot be too frequently or minutely studied by those who would

---

1. "If any does not provide for his own, and especially for those of his own house, he has denied the faith, and is worse than an unbeliever." 1 Timothy 5:8.
2. Proverbs 31:10-31.

attain to high degrees of female excellence.[1] The business of providing for the family, however, belongs chiefly to the husband. It is his to rise up early, to sit up late, to eat the bread of carefulness, and to drink, if necessary, the waters of affliction that he may earn a comfortable support for the domestic circle, *by the sweat of his brow.*[2] This is probably what the apostle meant when he enjoined us to *give honor to the wife as to the weaker vessel*[3]—the honor of maintenance, which she, in consequence of the weakness of her frame and the frequent infirmities which the maternal relation brings upon her, is not so well able to procure for herself.[4]

In general, it is for the benefit of a family that a married woman should devote her time and attention almost exclusively to the ways of her household: her place is in the center of domestic cares. What is gained by her in the shop, is oftentimes lost in the home, for want of the judicious superintendence of a mother and mistress of the house. Comfort and order, as well as money, are domestic wealth, and can these be rationally expected in the absence of female arrangement? The children

---

1. Likewise, if a godly woman should excel in all these things, then how much more so should a godly man; who, as head of the household, is primarily responsible for its welfare and provision.

2. Genesis 3:19.

3. "Husbands, dwell with them according to knowledge, giving honor to the wife, as to the weaker vessel, and as being heirs together of the grace of life, that your prayers be not hindered." 1 Peter 3:7.

4. "Peter ... says, 'Men, dwell with your wives according to knowledge,' (that is, according to the doctrine of Christ) 'giving reverence to the wife, as to the weaker vessel,' (that is, help her to bear her infirmities;) 'and as to them that are heirs also of the grace of life, that your prayers be not hindered.' In many things God has made the men stronger than the women, not to rage upon them and to be tyrants to them but to help them to bear their weakness. Therefore, be courteous to them and win them to Christ, and overcome them with kindness, that, of love, they may obey the ordinance that God has made between man and wife." William Tyndale, The Obedience of a Christian Man (1528).

always need a mother's eye and hand, and should always have them. Let the husband, then, have the care of providing and the wife, that of distributing to the necessities of the family. This is the rule of both reason and revelation.

And as Christ not only labored for his church during his abode upon earth but he made provision for its welfare when he departed from our world, in like manner should the husband take care of his wife. I never could understand the propriety of that custom, which is all too common, of men providing so much better for the children than they do for the mother in their wills. Does this look like a supreme love? Every man who raises a woman to the rank of his wife should take care, no matter how inferior her circumstances may have been before their marriage, to leave her in the situation into which he brought her. For it is indeed most cruel, to leave her to be deprived at once not only of her dearest earthly friend but of her usual means of comfortable subsistence.

A practical affection to a wife extends, however, to everything. It should manifest itself in the most delicate attention to her comfort and her feelings, in consulting her tastes, in concealing her failings, in never doing anything to degrade her, but everything to exalt her before her children and whomever may be employed under her, in acknowledging her excellences and commending her efforts to please him, and in meeting and even anticipating all her reasonable requests. In short, in doing all that ingenuity can devise for her happiness and general comfort.

Christ's Love was Unchangeable

Christ's love to his church was durable and unchangeable. *Having loved his own, he loved them to the end,*[1] without abatement or alteration. So should husbands love their wives[2] not only at the beginning, but to the end of their union, when the charms of beauty have fled before the withering influence of disease, when the energetic and lively frame has lost its elasticity and the step has become slow and faltering, when the wrinkles of age have succeeded the bloom of youth and the whole person seems rather the monument than the resemblance of what it once was. Has she not gained in mind what she has lost in exterior fascinations? Have not her mental graces flourished amidst the ruins of personal charms? If the youthful beauty has faded, have not the fruits of righteousness grown in the soul? If those blossoms have departed, on which the eye of youthful passion gazed with so much ardor, has it not been to give way to the ripe fruit of Christian excellence? The woman is not what she was, but the wife, the mother, the Christian, are better than they were. For an example of conjugal love in all its power and excellence, point me not to the bride and bridegroom displaying, during the first month of their union, all the watchfulness and tenderness of affection, but let me look upon the husband and wife of fifty, whose love has been tried over the course and through the changes of a quarter of a century and who, through this period and by the vicissitudes of time, have grown in attachment and esteem, and whose affection, if not

1. John 13:1.
2. "Rejoice with the wife of your youth. As a loving hind and a pleasant doe, let her breasts satisfy you at all times; and be always ravished with her love." Proverbs 5:18-19.

glowing with all the fervid heat of a midsummer's day, is still like the sunshine of an October noon, warm and beautiful, as reflected amidst the tints of autumn.

Love Your Wife as Your Own Body

Before I conclude this view of a husband's special duty, I must turn your attention to another rule of the husband's affection which is laid down for him by the apostle: "*So ought husbands to love their wives as their own bodies; he that loves his wife loves himself.*"[1] A man's children are parts of himself but his wife *is* himself, for, "*they two shall become one flesh.*"[2] "*This is his duty and the measure of it, too, which is so plain, that if he understands how he treats himself, nothing needs to be added concerning his demeanor towards her; for what mighty care does he take of his body and uses it with a delicate tenderness, and cares for it in all contingencies, and watches to keep it from all evils, and studies to make fair provisions for it, and is very often led by its inclinations and desires, and never contradicts its appetites, except when they are evil, and then also not without some trouble and sorrow!*" So let a man love his wife as his own body.

Is it necessary to apply the force of motives to produce an appropriate attention to such a duty? If so, I appeal to your sense of honor. Husbands, call to recollection the constancy of attentiveness and the tender attention, by which you won the affection and confidence of the woman, who forsook her father and mother, and the

---

1. "So ought husbands to love their wives as their own bodies; he that loves his wife loves himself. For no one ever hated his own flesh, but nourishes and cherishes it, even as the Lord does the church." Ephesians 5:28-29.
2. "A man shall leave his father and mother, and shall be joined to his wife, and they two shall be one flesh." Ephesians 5:31.

home of her childhood, to find a resting place for her heart in your attachment. Will you falsify the vows you pledged and disappoint the hopes you raised? It is accounted a disgraceful stigma on a man's reputation to forfeit the pledges he made to a lover. Oh, how much more dishonorable then, to forget those of a husband! That man has disgraced himself who furnishes just occasion to the partner of his days, to draw with a sigh a contrast between the affectionate attention she received as a lover and then as a wife.

I urge affection to a wife, by the recollection of that solemn moment when, in the presence of heaven and earth, you bound yourself by all the grave formalities of a kind of oath, to throw open and to keep open your heart, as the fountain of her earthly happiness, and to devote your whole life to the promotion of her welfare.

I appeal to your regard of justice. You have sworn away yourself to her and are no longer your own. You have no right to that individual and separate, and independent kind of life, which would lead you to seek your happiness in opposition to or neglect of hers. You two are *one flesh*.

Humanity puts in its claim on behalf of your wife. It is in your power to do more for her happiness or misery than any other being in the universe but God himself. An unkind husband is a tormentor of the first class.[1] His victim can never elude his grasp, nor go beyond the reach of his cruelty, until she is kindly released by the king of terrors, who, in this instance, becomes to her an angel of light and conducts her to the grave as to a shelter from her oppressor. For such a woman there

1. "I think, both in justice and compassion, [all] should unite in despising the man who dares to use a deserving woman ill, because he has not a heart to value her." John Newton, The Works, Letters to a Wife.

is no rest on earth, for the destroyer of her peace has her ever in his power and she is always in his presence or in the fear of it. The circumstances of every place and every day furnish him with the occasions of cruel neglect or unkindness and, it might be fairly questioned whether there is to be found on earth a case of greater misery, except it be that of a wretch tortured by remorse and despair, than a woman whose heart daily withers under the cold looks, the chilling words, and the repulsive actions of a husband who does not love. Such a man is a murderer,[1] although he escapes in this world the murderer's doom. He, by a refinement of cruelty, employs years in conducting his victim to her end, by the slow process of a lingering death.

If nothing else can prevail, interest should,[2] for no man can hate his wife without hating himself, for *she is his own flesh*.[3] Love, like mercy, is a double blessing, and hatred, like cruelty, is a double torment. We cannot love a worthy object without rejoicing within the very warmth of our own affection. Next to the supreme regard we cherish towards God and which it is impossible to exercise and not hold communion with angels in the joys of heaven, connubial love is the most beatifying passion, and to transform this into unkindness is to open, at the very center of our soul,

---

1. "Whoever hates his brother is a murderer, and you know that no murderer has eternal life abiding in him." 1 John 3:15.

2. "This have you done again, covering the alter of the Lord with tears, with weeping, and with crying out; insomuch that he does not regard the offering anymore, or receive it with good will at your hand. Yet you say, Wherefore? Because the Lord has been witness between you and the wife of your youth, against whom you have dealt treacherously: yet is she your companion and, the wife of your covenant. And did he not make one? Yet has he the residue of the spirit. And why one? That he might seek a godly seed. Therefore take heed to your spirit, and let none deal treacherously against the wife of his youth." Malachi 2:13-15.

3. Ephesians 5:28-29.

a source of poison, which, before it exudes to torture others, is the tormentor of our own selves.

CHAPTER 5
Special Duties of a Wife

CHAPTER 5
Special Duties of a Wife

"Oh! Blest with temper, whose unclouded ray
Can make tomorrow cheerful as today;
She, who never answers until a husband cools,
Or, if she rules him, never shows she rules;
Charms by accepting, by submitting sways;
Yet has her humor most when she obeys."

Wives Submit to Your Husbands

The first duty, which I would mention, is subjection. *"Wives, submit yourselves to your own husbands, as to the Lord. For the husband is head of the wife, even as Christ is head of the church: and he is the Savior of the body. Therefore, as the church is subject to Christ, so let the wives be to their own husbands in everything."*[1] The same thing is also enjoined in the Epistle to the Colossians.[2] Peter harmonizes with Paul and, in the same vein, says: *"Wives, be in subjection to your own husbands."*[3] Before I discuss the kind of subjection that is commanded here, it is necessary to state the nature of the authority to which subjection is to be yielded.

1. Ephesians 5:22-24.   2. Colossians 3:18.   3. 1 Peter 3:1.

Nature of a Husband's Authority

A husband's authority is such as is compatible with true religion and the claims of God—for no man has a right to enjoin and no woman is bound to obey any demand or direction that is in opposition to the letter or spirit of the Bible. A husband's authority is such as is consonant with sound reason: its injunctions must all be reasonable. For, it is against the Scriptures to expect a wife to become the slave of folly any more than of cruelty. A husband's authority is such that it accords with the idea of companionship.[1] It was very beautifully observed by an ancient writer that when Adam endeavored to shift the blame of his transgression onto his wife, he did not say, "the woman you gave *to* me." No such thing—she is not counted as his goods, nor his possessions, and she is not reckoned as his servant. But he said, "the woman you gave *to be with me,*"[2] that is, to be my partner and the companion of my joys and sorrows.

Let conjugal authority be founded upon love,[3] let it never be exercised in opposition to revelation or reason,[4]

1. "She is your companion and, the wife of your covenant." Malachi 2:14.
2. Genesis 3:12.
3. "Love suffers long and is kind; love does not envy; love does not vaunt itself, is not puffed up; does not behave unseemly, does not seek its own, is not provoked, thinks no evil; does not rejoice in iniquity, but rejoices in the truth; bears all things, believes all things, hopes all things, endures all things. Love never fails." 1 Corinthians 13:4-8.
4. The Bible furnishes us with abundant illustrations of this truth. The account of Abigail and Nabal is an example of one circumstance in which a wife must contradict the decision of her husband (1 Samuel 25). Likewise, the story of the two prophets illustrates the perilous result of heeding any instruction opposed to God's commands (1 Kings 13). Again, King Saul's command, which would have been the death of his son Jonathan, if it were not for the prevailing argument of those of sound reason (1 Samuel 14:24-45). Each example plainly shows us that no earthly authority can overturn God's revealed truth.

and let it be regulated by the idea of companionship. Then there will be no need of particular rules for its guidance. For, within these limits, it can never degenerate into tyranny and it can never oppress those who are subject to it.[1] To such an authority any woman can bow without being degraded and be humble to it without being humiliated, for its *yoke is easy and its burden is light.*[2] In the governing of every community, there must be precedence vested somewhere, there must be an ultimate authority and a last and highest court from which decisions are not to be appealed. This applies to the government of a family, which finds its headship in the father, just as it applies to the government of society, which finds its headship in the governor.

In every family, then, this responsibility is vested in the husband. The husband is the head,[3] the lawgiver, and the one that rules the household. In all matters touching the little world inside the household, he is to direct, although indeed, not without taking counsel with his wife, for, she is his *"helpmeet,"* his closest counselor and assistant. Yet, in all discordancy of view, he is to decide and he must take responsibility for the decision. The wife should yield to his decision and yield with grace and cheerfulness.[4] No man should resign his authority as the head of the family and no woman should wish

1. "All things whatsoever you would that men should do to you, do even to them, for this is the law and the prophets." Matthew 7:12.

2. Matthew 11:30.

3. "Wives, submit yourselves to your own husbands as to the Lord. For the husband is the head of the wife, even as Christ is head of the church: and he is the Savior of the body. Therefore, as the church is subject to Christ, so let the wives be to their own husbands in everything." Ephesians 5:22-24.

4. "A cheerful subjection and a loving, reverential respect, are duties which Christian women owe their husbands." Matthew Henry, Commentary on the Bible.

him to do so. He may give up his preferences and yield to her wishes, but he must not abdicate his headship, nor resign his governance. This kind of usurping of a husbands authority is always contemptible; and it is one of the most offensive exhibitions of family disorder, when a husband is degraded into the slave of an overbearing and controlling wife. Such a woman looks contemptible even upon a throne.

Submission to Weak Husbands

I admit it is difficult for a sensible woman to submit to imbecility. Therefore, a woman must exercise the most sober and impartial consideration of a man's character before she unites herself to him. Yet, in cases where the union has already been formed, let her give the strongest proof of her good sense that her circumstances will allow her to offer, by making that concession to superiority of station, which there is no opportunity in her case to do to superiority of mind. With the utmost tact, let her take the greater care in her role as helpmeet, offering sound reason and using persuasion and solicitation. One of the finest scenes, ever to be presented in the domestic economy, is that of a sensible woman employing her talents and diplomacy, not to subvert, but to support the authority of a weak husband. A woman who prompts, but does not command, who persuades, but does not dictate, who influences, but does not compel, and who, after taking pains to conceal her beneficial interference, submits to the authority which she has both supported and guided.[1]

An opposite line of conduct is most mischievous. For, weakness, when placed in perpetual contrast with

---

1. "Every wise woman builds her house, but the foolish plucks it down with her hands." Proverbs 14:1.

superior judgment, is rarely blind to its own defects. And, as this consciousness of inferiority, when united with office, is always jealous, it is both watchful and resentful of any interference with its prerogative. There must be subjection then and, when it cannot be yielded to superior talents, because there are none, it must be conceded to superiority of station. However, let husbands be careful not to put the submission of their wives to too severe a test. For, it is hard, very hard, to obey an arrogant, rash, indiscreet, and foolish ruler.[1] *"If you will be the head, remember the head is not only the seat of government, but of knowledge. If you will have the management of the ship, see that a fool is not placed at the helm. Shall the blind offer themselves as guides?"*

Biblical Grounds for Submission

The grounds for submission are many and strong. Waiving all arguments regarding the comparative strength of mind with which the two sexes may be gifted, I refer my female friends to less questionable matters. Look at the creation: woman was made after the man, *"for Adam was formed first, then Eve."*[2] She was made out of man, *"for man is not of the woman, but the woman of the man."*[3] She was made for man: *"neither was the man created for the woman, but the woman for the man."*[4] Look at the fall: woman occasioned it: *"Adam was not deceived, but the woman being deceived was in the transgression."*[5] She was thus punished for it: *"Your desire shall be to your husband, and he shall rule over you."*[6] Look at her history. Have not the customs of all nations, both ancient and modern, savage and civilized, acknowledged

---

1. Others need to take care also to judge such relationships with caution, as the public eye and a jealous or resentful husband may offer an incomplete view into the affairs of the household (Proverbs 18:17).

2. 1 Timothy 2:13.   3. 1 Corinthians 11:8.   4. 1 Corinthians 11:9.

5. 1 Timothy 2:14.   6. Genesis 3:16.

her subordination? Look at the light in which this subject is placed in the New Testament. How strong is the language of the text, *"the husband is the head of the wife, even as Christ is the head of the church; and he is the Savior of the body. Therefore, as the church is subject to Christ, so let the wives be to their own husbands in everything."*[1]

Let me then, my respected female friends, admonish you meekly and with grace,[2] as you would submit to the authority of Christ and, as you would adorn the station that Providence has called you to occupy, as you would promote your own peace, the comfort of your husband and the welfare of your family, that you be subject in all things, not only to the wise and good, but also to the foolish and undeserving.[3] You may reason, as I have said before and you may remonstrate, but you must not frowardly rebel or refuse. Let it be your glory to feel how much you can endure, rather than despise the institutions of heaven or violate those engagements into which you voluntarily and so solemnly entered. Let your submission be characterized by cheerfulness

1. Ephesians 5:23-24.
2. "Teach the young women to be sober, to love their husbands, to love their children, to be discreet, chaste, keepers at home, good, obedient to their own husbands, that the Word of God be not blasphemed." Titus 2:4-5.
3. "Servants, be subject to your masters with all fear, not only to the good and gentle, but also to the froward. For this is thankworthy, if a man for conscience towards God endure grief, suffering wrongfully. For what glory is it, if, when you are buffeted for your faults, you take it patiently? But, if, when you do well, and suffer for it, you take it patiently, this is acceptable with God. For even to this were you called, because Christ also suffered for us, leaving us an example, that you should follow his steps: Who did not sin, neither was guile found in his mouth; who, when he was reviled, did not revile again; when he suffered, he did not threaten, but committed himself to him that judges righteously. ... Likewise you wives, be in subjection to your own husbands; that, if any do not obey the word, they also may without the word be won by the conduct of the wives, when they observe your chaste conduct coupled with fear." 1 Peter 2:18-3:2.

and not by reluctant sullenness. Let it not be preceded by a struggle, but yielded at once and forever. Let there be no holding out to the last extremity, and then only a mere compulsory surrender; but a voluntary, cheerful, undisputed, and unrevoked concession.

Wives Respect Your Husbands

Reverence, or respect, is another duty enjoined on the wife. *"Let the wife see that she respects her husband."*[1] This duty is closely allied to the last duty, but is still somewhat different. By respect, the apostle does not mean anything like slavish or servile homage, but that respect and deference which is due to one whom we are commanded to obey.

Show Respect by Your Words

Your respect will be evidenced by your words. For instance, in the way you talk *about* your husband, you will avoid everything that might lessen him in the esteem of others. You will avoid all exposure of his faults and minor weaknesses,[2] and all depreciation of his understanding and domestic rule. Such gossip is detestable and mischievous, for, can anything tend to irritate him more than to find that you have lowered him in the public's esteem?[3]

Your respect will also be displayed in the manner that you talk *to* him. *"Even as Sarah obeyed Abraham, calling him Lord."*[4] All flippant pertness, everything of a contemptuous consciousness of superiority,[5] of

1. Ephesians 5:33.
2. "He that covers a transgression seeks love." Proverbs 17:9.
3. "A virtuous woman is a crown to her husband, but she that causes shame is like rottenness in his bones." Proverbs 12:4.
4. 1 Peter 3:6.   5. "By pride comes contention." Proverbs 13:10.

dictation and command, of unnecessary contradiction, of obstinate and obtrusive disputing, of reactive and scolding accusation, of angry, reproachful complaint, of noisy and defiant remonstration, should be avoided.

Almost all domestic quarrels begin with words and it is usually within a woman's power to prevent them by causing *the law of kindness to dwell upon her lips,*[1] and calming the gusts of her husband's passion by those *soft answers, which turn away wrath.*[2]

A wife should be especially careful how she speaks to him, and of how she speaks in his presence, in the company of others, especially that of her own family and strangers. She must not talk him into silence, nor talk *at* him, nor say anything that is calculated to wound or degrade him, for, a sting inflicted in public is twice as charged with venom. She must not endeavor to eclipse him, to engross the attention of the company all to herself, or to reduce him to insignificance, so that he seems without value until she stands before him. This is not reverence and respect. On the contrary, she should do everything that is within her power to uphold his respectability and dignity in public esteem. And, indeed, her very mode of addressing him, when it shows the kindness of affection and the deference of respect, is eminently calculated to do this.

And if at any time he expresses himself in the language of reproof, even if that reproof is causeless or unjustly severe, let her be cautious not to forget her station, so as to be betrayed into a reactive or railing accusation,[3] a contemptuous silence, or a moody sullenness. I am

---

1. Proverbs 31:26.
2. "A soft answer turns away wrath, but grievous words stirs up anger." Proverbs 15:1.
3. "Michael the archangel, when contending with the devil he disputed about the body of Moses, dared not bring against him a railing accusation,

aware that it is difficult to show respect and reverence when there are no other grounds for it than mere station, just as it is easy to show respect when wisdom, dignity, and piety are present to support his claim to respect within the relationship. But in proportion to the difficulty of any virtuous action, is its excellence; and hers is indeed a superior virtue, who yields to the relationship of her husband that reverence, which he forbids her to pay him on account of his conduct.

Show Respect by Your Actions

A wife's respect will extend itself to her actions and will lead to a continual desire to please him in all things. It is assumed by the apostle, as an indisputable and general fact, that *the married woman cares about how she may please her husband.*[1] All her conduct should be founded upon this principle, to give him contentment and to increase his delight in her. Let her appear contented with her lot[2] and that will do much to make him content with his. On the other hand, nothing is more likely to generate discontent in his heart than the appearance of it in her.

Let her, by maintaining a cheerful good humor, diffuse an air of pleasantness within the home. Let her guard, as much as possible, against a gloomy and moody disposition, which causes her to move about with the silence and cloudiness of a phantom—for who would enjoy living in a house with such a person? She should always welcome him across his threshold with a smile and ever put forth all her ingenuity in studying how to please him, by consulting his wishes, by surprising him

---

but said, the Lord rebuke you." Jude 1:9. "Being reviled, we bless; being persecuted, we suffer it: being defamed, we entreat." 1 Corinthians 4:12-13.

1. 1 Corinthians 7:34.

2. "Be content with such things as you have." Hebrews 13.5.

occasionally with those unexpected devices of affection, which, though small in themselves, are the proofs of a mind intent upon the business of giving pleasure.

Endearing Power of Respect

The greater acts of reverent and respectful love are often regarded as matters of course and, as such, they make little impression. But, the lesser acts of attention, which are not part of the usual routine of conjugal duties or the everyday offices which may be relied upon with almost as much certainty as the coming of the hour they are to occupy, are as freewill offerings of an inventive and active affection. These extra tokens of respect and expressions of love, have a mighty power to attach a husband to his wife. They are the cords of love and the ties of a man's affection. In all her personal and domestic habits, then, her first care, next to that of pleasing God, must be to please him. By such means, she will hold and endear his heart to herself. For, his heart cannot wander away from her without carrying away her happiness with it and, once it has departed, cannot be restored by any power short of Omnipotence itself.

A Meek and Quiet Spirit

Meekness is mentioned in particular by the Apostle Peter, as a disposition that every wife is duty bound to cultivate. He has distinguished and honored this temperament by calling it *"the ornament of a meek and quiet spirit, which is of great price in the sight of God."*[1] If there are some virtues which preeminently suit the female character, meekness has a high place among them. No one stands in greater need of a meek

---

1. 1 Peter 3:4.

disposition than the female head of a family. For, if she is easy to provoke, either the insolence and disobedience of her children, the negligence and misconduct of those who are under her, or the sharp words of her husband, are sure to keep her in a state of irritation all day long.

And, oh, how trying is a quarrelsome woman! How odious is a brawling one! For, *"it is better to dwell in the wilderness, than with a contentious and angry woman."*[1] The Graces were females, says Mr. Jay; so also were the Furies. The influence that meekness has had on a family is sometimes astonishing—it has quenched the sparks and even the coals of anger and strife, which would otherwise have set the house on fire.[2] Meekness has subdued the tiger and the lion and led them away captive with the silken thread of love.

The strength of woman does not lie in resisting, but in yielding: her power is in her gentleness. There is more real defense and aggressive operation in one mild look and one soft tone, which disarms a foe, than there is in hours of flashing glances and angry words.[3] When, in the midst of domestic strife, she has been enabled to keep her temper calm,[4] the storm has often been scattered just as quickly as it arose. Her meekness has conducted away the dreadful flashes that threatened to destroy the home.

---

1. Proverbs 21:19; "Let all bitterness, and wrath, and anger, and clamor, and evil speaking, be put away from you, with all malice." Ephesians 4:31.

2. "The beginning of strife is like letting out water; therefore leave off contention, before there is quarreling." Proverbs 17:14.

3. "By long forbearance is a prince persuaded, and a soft tongue breaks the bone." Proverbs 25:15.

4. "He that is slow to wrath is of great understanding." Proverbs 14:29.

Modesty in Clothing & Appearance

Put on, then, *"the ornament of a meek and quiet spirit."*[1] Pay less attention to the decoration of your body and more attention to the decoration of your mind and character. Your beauty *is not to be that outward adorning of plaiting the hair, and of wearing of gold, or of putting on of apparel; but the hidden man of the heart, which is not corruptible.*[2] The language of another apostle speaking on this subject is no less striking: *"In like manner, also, I will that women adorn themselves in modest apparel, with shamefacedness and sobriety; not with broidered hair, or gold, or pearls, or costly array; but, which becomes women professing godliness, with good works."*[3] These both, writing as they were moved by the Holy Spirit and in such language as this, have denounced as improper and unbecoming to a profession of godliness, a taste for immodest,[4] expensive, or highly decorative adornment and dress.

This subject, therefore, is worthy of the most serious attention of all Christian women. By what sophistry can the words, much less, the spirit of these two passages of Scripture that are so plain and express in their terms be set aside? Yet, it is evident in the appearance of almost every congregation into which we could enter on a Sunday, that they *are* set aside.

---

1. 1 Peter 3:4.   2. 1 Peter 3:3-4.   3. 1 Timothy 2:9-10.

4. "The worst of all fashions are those which are evidently calculated to allure the eyes, and to draw the attention of our sex. Is it not strange that modest and even pious women should be seduced into a compliance even with these? Yet I have sometimes been in company with ladies of whose modesty I have no doubt, and of whose piety I entertain a good hope, when I have been embarrassed and at a loss which way to look. They are indeed noticed by the men, but not to their honour or advantage. The manner of their dress gives encouragement to vile and insidious men, and exposes

It is high time for Christian teachers to call women *"professing godliness"* back from their wanderings in the regions of fashionable folly, to the Holy Scriptures. For Scripture, it should be remembered, lays down a general law for regulating the adornment of the body, as well as that of the mind. I exhort you, then, that these passages of Scripture are still parts of revelation and, as such, they are still binding upon the conscience—if not, show me *where* they were cancelled.

I contend that Christian women should abstain from expensive, showy, and extravagant fashions in clothing and jewelry, and every sort of inappropriate personal decoration. I am not arguing for a sectarian costume, a religious uniform, or canonical shapes and colors—no, nothing of the kind, but for simplicity, neatness, and economy; for what the apostle calls modest apparel, shamefacedness, and sobriety; for the spirit of the passages if not the very letter; for a distinction between those who profess godliness, in their comparative inattention to such things, and those who make no such profession; for a proof that their minds are not so much engaged in these matters, as the minds of the people of the world are.

I am not for extinguishing taste, but for resisting the lawless dominion of folly under the name of fashion. I am not for calling back the age of Gothic barbarism or vulgarity, no, I will leave ample room for the cultivation of both taste and genius in every lawful department, but I am protesting against the desolating reign of vanity. I

them to dangerous temptations. This inconsiderate levity has often proved the first step into the road that leads to misery and ruin. They are pleased with the flattery of the worthless, and go on without thought, 'as a bird hastens to the snare, and knows not that it is for its life,' (Proverbs 7:23). But honest and sensible men regard their exterior as a warning signal, not to choose a companion for life from among persons of this light and volatile turn of mind." John Newton, The Works, On Female Dress.

am resisting the entrance of frivolity into the church of God. I am contending against the glaring inconsistency of rendering our religious assemblies like the audience convened in a theater.

The evils of an improper attention to dress are great and numerous. Much precious time is wasted on the study, arrangements, and decisions of this matter. The attention is drawn away from improving the mind and heart and made to focus on the decoration of the outward person.[1] The mind is easily filled with pride and vanity, and a deteriorating influence is set up against that which constitutes the true dignity of the soul. The love of display infects the character. Money is wasted that is needed for relieving the misery and improving the condition of mankind.[2] Examples are set for those who are less wealthy, in whom such a propensity is often mischievous in many ways.

I am aware there might be and there is said to be a particular pride in singularity, as well as in fashion: the pride of being covered with sober autumn tints, as well as of exhibiting the brilliant hues of the rainbow; the pride of quality and of texture, as well as of color and of form. I know this, and I do not justify the one

1. "A nice attention to dress will cost you much of what is more valuable than money—your precious time. It will too much occupy your thoughts and that at the seasons when you would wish to have them otherwise engaged. And it certainly administers fuel to that latent fire of pride and vanity, which is inseparable from our fallen nature, and is easily blown up into a blaze." John Newton, The Works, On Female Dress.

2. "There are likewise women, who, we would hope, are pious, and therefore, of course, benevolent. But an attachment to dress, and a desire to approach, as near as they can, to the standard of those who are their superiors in fortune, blunt their compassionate feelings, and deprive them of the usefulness, comfort, and honor, they might otherwise attain. The expense of their dress is so great, compared with the smallness of their income, that when they have decorated themselves to their mind, they have little or nothing to spare for the relief of the poor." Ibid.

more than I do the other—I condemn every kind, but, in any case, there is a little more dignity in the one kind than there is in the other. I leave opportunity for the distinctions of rank, for the inventions of true taste, and for the modest and unobtrusive displays of natural elegance and simple beauty. But I cannot allow the propriety of Christian women yielding themselves to the guidance of fashion, no matter how expensive, extravagant, or gaudy.

As for the employment of our artisans by the various changes in fashion, I have nothing to do with this in the face of an apostolic injunction. The silversmiths, who made shrines for the worshippers of Diana, might have pleaded the same objection against the preachers of the Gospel, who certainly did ruin their trade, as far as they were successful and the Gospel was received.[1] I am only speaking to professors of religion, who form so small a portion of society, that their abstinence from sinful fashions would do little to diminish the demand for workers in this industry and, even if their abstinence did much, let the artisans make up for it in some other way. What I contend for, then, is not inferiority or unvarying similarity, but neatness opposed to gaudiness, simplicity and comeliness opposed to extravagance, modesty opposed to indecency,[2] and economy opposed to expensiveness.

Whether what I contend for is characteristic of the age in which we live, let any spectator decide. I am anxious to see those who profess godliness displaying

---

1. Acts 19:24, etc.
2. "Abstain from all appearance of evil." 1 Thessalonians 5:22. "Do not imitate that which is evil, but that which is good." 3 John 1:11.
   "We are required to attend to the things that are lovely and of a good report (Philippians 4:8). Every wilful deviation from this rule is sinful. Why should a godly woman ... hazard a suspicion of her character, to please and imitate an ungodly world?" John Newton, The Works, On Female Dress.

a seriousness and spirituality, a dignity and sobriety of mind, a simplicity of habits, and a gravity of manners appropriate to their high and holy profession.[1] And all this united with an economy in their personal spending, which will leave them a greater amount at their disposal for relieving the miseries and promoting the happiness of their fellow creatures.

But, perhaps, after all, many women may plead that the showiness and expense of their attire is more to please their husbands than themselves, but even this must have its limits. I truly pity the folly of any man who concerns himself too much in the arrangement of his wife's wardrobe and appearance. Who would rather see her go about in all the gorgeousness of exquisite apparel, to display herself in the houses of their friends, rather than, in dignified neatness, to visit the homes of the poor as a messenger of mercy. Who rejoices more to contemplate her moving through the circles of fashion, being the admiration of one sex and the envy of the other, than to see her set upon a radiant course of benevolence, adorned in inexpensive simplicity and with the savings from her personal expenses, clothing the naked, feeding the hungry, healing the sick, and thus bringing upon herself the blessings of him that was ready to perish and causing the widow's heart to sing for joy.

All Beauty Perishes, Except Inward Grace

Let it be remembered that not only the beautification but the person that it adorns is corruptible. Accidents may distort the finest form, diseases may fade the

---

1. "Whatever you do, do all to the glory of God. Give no offence, either to the Jews or to the Gentiles or to the church of God." 1 Corinthians 10:31-32. "For you were bought with a price, therefore glorify God in your body and in your spirit, which are God's," 1 Corinthians 6:20.

loveliest coloring, time may disfigure the smoothest surface, and death, the spoiler of all beauty, may work such an awful and appalling change, that even the most impassioned admirers will turn away. How soon will every other dress be displaced by the shroud and every other decoration removed to make way for the flowers that are laid upon the body, as if to hide the deformity of death.

However, the graces of the heart and the beauties of the character are imperishable. Let a wife be continually seeking to put on such, *"for she that has a wise husband must entice him to an eternal dearness, by the veil of modesty and the robes of chastity, the ornaments of meekness and the jewels of faith and charity; her brightness must be her purity and she must shine roundabout with sweetness and friendship, and then she shall be pleasant while she lives and longed for when she dies."*

Economy & Thrift in Spending

Economy and order in the management of her personal and household expenses are the obvious duty of a wife. You are to preside over the direction of household affairs and much of the prosperity and comfort of that little community will depend upon your skilful and prudent arrangements.[1] There is a disposition in this age, in all classes of society, to come as closely as possible to the habits of those who are wealthier. The poor imitate the middle class and the middle class copies the upper class. A showy, luxurious, and expensive taste is almost universally cherished and is displayed in innumerable instances where there are little or no means to support it.

---

1. Proverbs 31:10-31.

A large house, a country residence, expensive furniture, luxury transportation, a staff of servants, and large parties are the goal of many whose creditors pay for everything. Christian families are in imminent peril of worldly conformity in this present day and the line of separation between Christians and the world is fast fading. It is true, they are not gamblers, they do not frequent the theaters or the dance halls, and perhaps they have no evening revelries, but this is all. For, many are as anxious about the splendor of their furniture, the fashionableness of their habits, and the expensiveness of their entertainments, as the vainest worldling can be.

Now, a wife has great influence in either hindering or promoting all of this. It has been thought that this increasing disposition for domestic display and extravagance is to be chiefly attributed to female vanity. Women are generally seen as the presiding genius over such a scene; she receives the praise and compliment for it and she is therefore under the strongest temptation to promote it. However, let her consider how little all of this has to do with the true happiness of her family, even in its most prosperous state. And let her consider how a recollection of it only aggravates the misery of adversity when a reversal of fortune occurs. Oh! To be found in debt for fine clothes or furniture; to have it said that her extravagance helped ruin her husband; to want that money now for food that was previously wasted on luxury; and to hear the whispered reproach of having injured others by her own thoughtless spending!

Avoid these miseries, my female friends. Do not go on to prepare a sour mixture to make the already bitter cup of adversity even more bitter. Endeavor to acquire a skillfulness in household management, a frugality and prudence, a love of order and neatness, and a middle course between crudeness and luxury that is suitable to your station in life and to your Christian profession.[1] Endeavour to establish an economy that will leave you more to spare for the cause of God and the miseries of man. Curb, rather than stimulate, the taste of your husband for expense: tell him that it is not necessary for your happiness nor for the comfort of your family. Draw him away from impulsive and unnecessary indulgences to the intellectual improvement, moral cultivation, and religious instruction of your children. Let knowledge and piety be cultivated.[2] Let good sense and well-formed habits order all things. Let harmony and mutual love be the sources of your domestic pleasures. For what is the splendor of furniture, dress, or entertainments compared to these?

A Mother's Duty, A Keeper at Home

A wife should be most attentive to all that concerns the welfare and comfort of her children. For this purpose, she must be a keeper at home. *"Teach the young women to be sober, to love their husbands, to love their children, to be discreet, chaste, keepers at home."*[3] How can the duties that fall upon the female head of a family be discharged well, if she is not a keeper at home? I have already discussed this in a previous chapter, but its importance will justify my returning to the subject. How many things does she have to attend to, how many cares to maintain, and how many activities to support when there is a young family. Whoever else may have leisure for gossiping, she has none. Whoever else may be found

---

1. "Give me neither poverty nor riches; feed me with food convenient for me: lest I be full, and deny you, and say, Who is the Lord? Or lest I be poor, and steal, and take the name of my God in vain." Proverbs 30:8-9.

2. "Receive my instruction, and not silver; and knowledge rather than choice gold. For wisdom is better than rubies; and all the things that may be desired are not to be compared to it." Proverbs 8:10-11.

3. Titus 2:4-5. "Keepers at home" may also be rendered "homemakers."

wandering from house to house, hearing or telling some interesting thing, she must not.[1]

A mother's place is in the midst of her family and a mother's duties are in the care of her family. Nothing can excuse a neglect of these and yet, we often see such neglect. Some women are the literary type, and the welfare of the household is neglected for books. Not that I would debar a woman from the luxury of reading, far from it, but her taste for literature must be kept within due bounds and not be allowed to interfere with her household duties. No husband can be pleased to see a book in his wife's hands, while the house is in confusion and the children's comfort is not provided for.[2] Much less should a taste for company be allowed to draw a wife too much away from the sphere of her care and duties. To be *wandering from house to house* in the morning or to be out until a late hour attending some party, evening after evening while the family is left to themselves at home, or in the care of others, is certainly disgraceful.

Even attention to the public duties of religion must be regulated by a due regard to domestic claims. I am aware that many are apt to use domestic claims as an excuse for neglecting the public means of grace almost entirely: the gathering place is unfrequented, sermons are unheard, sacramental seasons, and all other religious meetings are given up for an all-absorbing attention to household affairs. This is one extreme. The other is such a devotedness to religious meetings that the needs of a sick family, the cries of a hungry infant, or the

---

1. 1 Timothy 5:13.
2. In our modern era, the more pertinent examples would be, of course, the television, telephone, and internet; and even the taxing demand of culture that would insist all women work outside the home, or be subject to the accusation of ignorance, laziness, or a lack of self-esteem.

circumstances of some extraordinary case of family care are not allowed to have any force in detaining a mother from attending a weekday sermon, a prayer meeting, or the anniversary of some public institution.

It is no honor to religion, under such circumstances, for a wife to be seen in the church. Duties cannot be in opposition to each other and, at such times, her duty is at home. It must always be distressing for a husband, upon his returning to a scene of domestic confusion and seeing a neglected child sick in bed, to be told that the mother is attending a sermon or public meeting. There is a great need for watchfulness in this present age, when female agency is in such demand, lest attention to public institutions and responsibilities outside the home should injuriously interfere with the duties of a wife and a mother.

I know very well that a diligent woman and a woman of some resource may, through well developed habits of order, punctuality, and dispatch, so arrange her more immediate and direct duties at home, as to allow for sufficient leisure time to assist the noble entities that solicit her patronage, without neglecting her husband or children. However, where this cannot be done, where resource is lacking, and where even the best of order cannot allow it, no society, whether humane or religious, should be allowed to take her away from what is, after all, her first and more appropriate sphere. She must be *a keeper at home,* if anything there demands her presence.

These things are the leading duties of a wife. Motives of a very high and sacred character may be offered for a diligent performance of them. Her own comfort and that of her husband is, of course, vitally connected with a fulfillment of her obligations. The welfare of her children is likewise deeply involved. Then her character shines forth with peculiar sparkle. A good wife and mother is a high attainment in female excellence, it is woman in her brightest glory.[1]

An Unconverted Husband

There is one more consideration of supreme importance, mentioned by the apostle, to which I will direct your attention. *"Likewise you wives, be in subjection to your own husbands; that, if any do not obey the word, they also may without the word be won by the conduct of the wives, when they observe your chaste conduct coupled with fear."*[2] A powerful and yet tender consideration! Mark, my female friends, the eulogy implied by the apostle regarding your sex, where he seems to take it for granted that if one party is destitute of religion, it is the husband. And facts prove that this assumption was correct.

Religion flourishes most among the female portion of our species. In our congregations and in our churches, the greater numbers are women. Can we account for this by natural causes? Partly. Women are more at home and, therefore, more within the reach of the means of grace. They are more susceptible—they are less exposed to those temptations that harden the heart through the deceitfulness of sin. And they are subject to more affliction, which softens the heart and prepares it for the word of the Gospel. Yet, all this is not enough, for without divine grace all these advantages avail nothing. Therefore, we must resolve that this is due to divine

---

1. "Her children rise up, and call her blessed; her husband also, and he praises her. Many daughters have done virtuously, but you excel them all. Favor is deceitful, and beauty is vain; but a woman that fears the Lord, she shall be praised. Give her the fruit of her hands, and let her own works praise her in the gates." Proverbs 31:28-31.

2. 1 Peter 3:1-2.

purposes, divine interjection, and the arrangements of divine wisdom.

Female influence in all civilized states is great and God has generally made much use of this wherever the Gospel has come, as one of the means for spreading religion. He pours his grace on them that their influence may be employed on others, especially their husbands and children. If, then, in any case, a Christian woman is united to an unconverted man, she must cherish and display a deep, tender, and judicious concern for his salvation, for, *"what do you know, oh wife, whether you shall save your husband?"*[1] I would not in any way whatsoever encourage unequal marriages.[2] I would not have anyone attempt the doubtful and dangerous experiment of marrying an irreligious man in the hope of converting him. In such cases, the conversion is often the other way around.[3] However, where the union is *already* formed, there, I say, nourish an anxiety regarding his salvation and employ every discreet effort for his eternal welfare.

Many instances have occurred in which the wife has saved her unbelieving husband. She has drawn him, with the cords of a tender and judicious love, to a consideration of the subject of personal religion. Think of the value of a soul and of the inexpressible glory of being the instrument of its salvation. Oh! To be the means of saving the soul of your husband! Think how it will strengthen the bond that unites you on earth and in time, and sanctify and sweeten it. Adding, at the same

1. 1 Corinthians 7:16.
2. "Do not be unequally yoked together with unbelievers: for what fellowship has righteousness with unrighteousness?" 2 Corinthians 6:14. See also Chapter 1, Forming the Marriage Union.
3. "The righteous is more excellent than his neighbor, but the way of the wicked seduces them." Proverbs 12:26. "Do not be deceived: evil communications corrupt good manners." 1 Corinthians 15:33.

time, a tie to your union, by which you will not lose one another in the valley of the shadow of death, but be reunited as kindred spirits in heaven and throughout all eternity, although not as man and wife.[1]

Think, oh wife, of the happiness—the honor that awaits you. What is the triumph you have acquired in him by your charms, compared with the victory you will obtain in him by your religion? What pleasures will accompany you for the remainder of your days! Now you are of *"one heart and one mind"* and now you *"take sweet counsel together."* The privileged language of prayer is now *"Our Father."*[2] In every motion made to go and seek the Lord of Hosts there is a ready acceptance: *"I will go also."* And what will be your *joy and crown of rejoicing*[3] in that day, when, before the assembly of men and angels,[4] he will say, "Oh blessed be the Providence which attached us in the world and has still more perfectly united us in this! The woman you gave to be with me did not lead me into temptation and sin but to the tree of life."[5]

Witnessing to an Unconverted Husband

Yet, how is this solicitude to be employed? The apostle tells us that they may *"be won by the conduct of the wives, when they observe your chaste conduct coupled with fear."*[6] Your religion must be seen embodied in your whole character and conduct. It must commend itself to their judgment by what they perceive as sincere. It must be consistent, for a lack of consistency, no matter how earnest it may appear in many respects and at many times, will produce disgust. You must *let your light so shine before them, that they, seeing your good works, may*

1. "For in the resurrection they neither marry, nor are given in marriage, but are as the angels of God in heaven." Matthew 22:30.

2. Matthew 6:9.   3. 1 Thessalonians 2:19.   4. Hebrews 12:22-24.
5. Revelation 22:2.   6. 1 Peter 3:1-2.

glorify God.[1] You must always appear invested with all the beauty of a lovely example, which, although you may be silent in respect to your tongue, is living eloquence.

Your religion must diffuse its sparkle over your whole character and impress itself most deeply upon your relationship as a wife and a mother. It must be a continually refreshed motivation for all the respect, reverence, devotedness, and meekness that is required of a wife and mother and it must motivate you to carry every conjugal and maternal virtue to the highest degree of perfection. It must be attended with the most profound humility, for, if there is any spiritual pride, any conscious and obvious sense of superiority, anything approaching a pharisaic temperament, which says, "Stand aside, I am holier than you," anything like contempt towards your husband as an unconverted sinner, you will excite a deep-rooted prejudice, not only against religion, but against yourself. Religion will be hated by him for your sake and you for religion's sake.

When you venture to speak to him about the subject of piety, it should be as far away as possible from all lecturing, all dictation, all reproach, all conscious superiority; and with all possible tenderness, meekness, humility, and persuasive affection. Never talk to him of his state in the presence of others and never talk *at* him. Nor is it likely to accomplish the end you have in view, to weary him by continually pressing the matter. Many defeat their own end by an incessant introduction of the subject and sometimes with an asperity that increases the revulsion, which its very harshness is calculated, in such a mind, to produce. An occasional hint, and that of the most tender, respectful, and delicate kind, is all

1. Matthew 5:16.

that you should attempt, and then leave your example to speak for itself and religion. Occasionally, you may put an instructive volume in his path and, when opportunity offers, solicit his perusal of it.

Do not bring your religious friends around you too much, so as to annoy him. And, as much as is possible, keep those friends away who may have less discretion than the rest, confining yourself to the most judicious and best-informed of them. Never rudely interfere with his pursuits, his reading, or his company, although they may not be what you can cordially approve. Until he is enlightened from above, he will not see the evil of these things and to attempt to interrupt him in any other way than by the mildest and most respectful remonstration, will only do harm.

If he wishes to draw you away from the high pursuit of eternal life, you are not, of course, to yield to his persuasion in this case, nor to concede in anything, where your conscience is decidedly concerned in the matter. You must be firm, but mild. One concession granted by you would only lead to another. Still, even in this extremity, your resistance of his attempts to interfere with your religion must be maintained in all the meekness of wisdom and must be attended with fresh efforts to please him in all things that are lawful. Many a persecuting husband has been subdued, if not to religion, yet to kinder conduct, by the meek and uncomplaining temperament of his wife. If such a line of conduct, however, should subject you to reproach, anger, and persecution, a most painful and by no means an uncommon situation,[1] you must possess your soul

---

1. "Do you suppose that I am come to give peace on earth? I tell you, no; but rather division. For from now on there shall be five in one house divided, three against two, and two against three." Luke 12:51-52.

in patience,[1] and commit your way to him that judges righteously.[2]

1. Luke 21:19.

2. Women who are in this circumstance need to hold, as a treasure in their hearts, this word of exhortation and promise: "For even to this were you called, because Christ also suffered for us, leaving us an example, that you should follow his steps: Who did not sin, neither was guile found in his mouth; who, when he was reviled, did not revile again; when he suffered, he did not threaten, but committed himself to him that judges righteously." (1 Peter 2:21-23). For, to posses the soul in patience (Luke 21:19) is to look for all the fruits of righteousness and the evident tokens of a lively faith in all the trials of life.

"Take, my brethren, the prophets, who have spoken in the name of the Lord, for an example of suffering affliction, and of patience. Behold, we count them happy which endure. You have heard of the patience of Job, and have seen the end of the Lord; that the Lord is very pitiful, and of tender mercy." James 5:10-11.

CHAPTER 6
Conclusion

CHAPTER 6
Conclusion

To conclude, let us all seek after more of the spirit of true religion—the spirit of faith, hope, and prayer. A faith that truly believes the Word of God and looks habitually to the cross of Christ, by which we obtain salvation, and to the eternal world where we shall fully and forever enjoy it. A hope that lives in the expectation and desire of *glory, honor, immortality, and eternal life,*[1] and a spirit of prayer that leads us daily and hourly to the *throne of divine grace,*[2] for all that assistance which we need from the Holy Spirit, not only for the duties we have in relation to the coming world, but also for those which fall upon us in consequence of our relation to this world. *"Godliness is profitable unto all things, having promise of the life that now is, and of that which is to come."*[3] The same principle of divine grace that unites us to God will bind us closer to each other.

Religion contains in it not only the seeds of immortal virtues, but also those that are mortal. Not only the buds of excellences that are to flourish in the temple of heaven, but also those that grow up in the house of our pilgrimage upon earth, to enliven with their beauty and to refresh the family circle with their fragrance. A good

1. Romans 2:7.   2. Hebrews 4:16.   3. 1 Timothy 4:8.

Christian *cannot* be a bad husband or father and, as this is equally true in everything, he who has the most piety will shine the most in all the relationships of life.[1]

A Bible placed between man and wife as the basis of their union, the rule of their conduct, and the model of their spirit will make up for many differences between them, comfort them under many crosses, guide them through many straits, wherein flesh and blood is confounded and at a loss, support them in their last sad parting from one another and reunite them in that happy world where they shall remain forever.

"Those married pairs that live as remembering that they must part again and give an account of how they treated themselves and each other will, upon the day of their death, be admitted to glorious espousals and, when they live again, be married to their Lord and partake of his glories. All those things that now please us will pass from us or we from them, but those things that concern eternal life are as permanent as the numbers of eternity. And although at the resurrection there will be no relation of husband and wife and no marriage will be celebrated but the marriage of the Lamb, yet then it will be remembered how men and women passed through this state, which is a symbol of that. And from this sanctified union, all holy pairs will pass on to the spiritual and eternal, where love will be their portion and joys will crown their heads, and they will lie in the bosom of Jesus and in the heart of God, unto eternal ages."

"Far, far beyond the reach of mortal ken,
No eye has seen it, nor has human pen

---

1. "Perkins said: 'Though a man is endued with excellent gifts, hears the Word with reverence and receives the sacrament, yet if he does not practise the duties of his calling, all is sheer hypocrisy.'" Thomas Watson, The Godly Man's Picture (1666).

Portrayed the glories of that world above,
Whose very atmosphere is holy love!

There Christians, who in union dwelt on earth,
Heirs of its mansions by celestial birth,
In blest society shall meet and blend
In love and fellowship that never end.

Oh! It will be passing sweet, to meet the friend
We loved on earth, and there together bend
Before the throne eternal, and rehearse
Its untold glories in exalted verse.

To walk in company the golden streets,
To sit, but not apart, on shining seats;
To trace the beauties of each dazzling gem,
Or pluck the fruit of some unfading stem!

To sip the waters of the sparkling fount,
To crop the flowers that deck the holy mount,
To breath the fragrance of the balmy gale,
Or on the crystal river spread the sail!

But most to adore the wonders of his grace,
To see the unveiled splendors of his face,
Who brought us with a price immense, unknown,
And raised us from a prison to a throne!"

FINIS

BONUS SERMON
Right to Divorce & Remarriage in the Case of Adultery

by
John Owen

1616-1683, English Puritan Preacher

2010 Edition
Modernized and edited from the 1862 Edition

Hail & Fire
www.hailandfire.com

BONUS SERMON
Right to Divorce & Remarriage in the Case of Adultery

by
John Owen
1616-1683, English Puritan Preacher

It is confessed by all that adultery is a just and sufficient ground for divorce between married persons.

Some say this type of divorce consists in a complete dissolution *"vinculi matrimonialis"*[1] and as such removes the marriage relationship entirely, so that the innocent spouse who is divorcing or procuring the divorce is at liberty to marry again.

Others say that this divorce is only a separation *"a mensa et thoro"*[2] and, therefore, it does not and should not entirely dissolve the marriage relationship.[3]

I am, however, of the first judgment; for:

1. *vinculi matrimonialis:* Latin for 'of the matrimonial bond.'
2. *a mensa et thoro:* Latin for 'of table and bed'; in law, a separation without dissolution of the marriage.
3. One would think heresies of this kind and related to this topic were entirely unheard of today, as the Bible is so readily accessible to anyone

First, the divorce *"a mensa et thoro"* only, is not a true divorce, but rather a mere fiction of a divorce, which is of no use in this case, nor is it lawful to be made use of either by the law of nature or the law of God; for:

1. It is, as stated, only a recent invention and has had no actual usage in the world, nor was it heard of in more ancient times. For even those of the Roman Catholic Church who assert it, do grant that divorces by the law of nature and under the Old Testament, were *"a vinculo;"*[1] and, therefore, this so called divorce—which indeed makes no alteration to the moral relationships and duties of marriage, but only directs their performance—they would impose only upon the grace and state of the Gospel.

2. It is deduced from a fiction, namely, that marriage among Christians is a sacrament and, therefore, of such signification as renders it indissolvable. For this reason they would have marriage take place only among believers, the rest of mankind being left to their natural right and privilege. But this is a fiction and, as such, in various cases they make use of it.

Secondly, a divorce perpetual *"a mensa et thoro"* only, is in no way useful to mankind, but is hurtful and noxious; for:

1. It would constitute a new condition or state of life, wherein it is not possible for a man to either lawfully have a wife or lawfully not have a wife.

---

seeking out the truth of this matter. Remarkably, however, there are if fact preachers today who corrupt this simple truth. The publisher has even witnessed a pastor admonish his massive non-denominational congregation to get right with God, by returning to their first spouse, even if they were already remarried and had children within that marriage, and irrespective of the occasion of the divorce, as the pastor himself was not convinced that adultery was sufficient cause.

1. *a vinculo:* Latin for 'from the bond.'

Yet, in one or the other of these two states every man capable of the state of wedlock is and must be, whether he wills it or not. For, as things may be circumstantiated, a man may be absolutely bound in conscience not to receive her back again who was justly repudiated for adultery, nor can he take a new wife under this fictional divorce. But into such a state God calls no man.

2. It may, and probably will, drive a man to the necessity of sinning: for suppose he does not have the gift of self-control, it is the express will of God that he should marry for his relief;[1] yet on the supposition of this fictional divorce, he sins if he remarries, and in that, he sins if he does not remarry.

Thirdly, it is unlawful; for if the bond of marriage abides, the relationship still continues. This relationship is the foundation of all mutual duties and while the relationship continues, no one can dispense of or prohibit the performance of those duties. If a woman does continue in the relationship as a wife to the man, she may claim the duties of marriage from him. Separation is lawful by consent for a season,[1] or upon

---

1. "It is good for a man not to touch a woman. Nevertheless, to avoid fornication, let every man have his own wife, and let every woman have her own husband. Let the husband render to the wife due benevolence: and likewise also the wife to the husband. The wife does not have power of her own body, but the husband: and likewise also the husband does not have power of his own body, but the wife. Do not defraud one another, except, it be with consent for a time, that you may give yourselves to fasting and prayer; and come together again, that Satan does not tempt you for your lack of self-control. But I speak this by permission, and not of commandment. For I would that all men were even as, I myself. But every man has his proper gift of God, one, after this manner, and another after that. I say therefore to the unmarried and widows, It is good for them if they abide even as I. But if they cannot contain, let them marry: for it is better to marry than to burn." 1 Corinthians 7:9.

other occasions that may hinder the actual discharge of conjugal duties, but to make the obligation of such duties void, while the relationship continues, is against the law of nature and the law of God. This fictional divorce, therefore, purporting that the relationship of man and wife remains, but no mutual duties arise from it, is unlawful.

Fourthly, the light of nature never directed us to this kind of divorce. Marriage is an ordinance of the law of nature and in the light and reason of nature there is no intimation of any such practice. Nature still directs that those who may justly put away their wives may marry others. Hence some, as the ancient Grecians and afterwards, the Romans, allowed the husband to put the adulteress to death. This among the Romans was changed *"lege Julia,"*[1] but the offence was still made capital. In the place thereof, afterward, divorce took place purposely to give the innocent person liberty to remarry. So that this kind of divorce is but a fiction.

The first opinion, therefore, is according to truth; for:

First, that which dissolves the form of marriage and destroys all the forms of marriage also dissolves the bond of marriage. For, take away the form and end of any moral relationship and the relationship itself ceases. This is done by adultery and a divorce ensuing thereupon. For, the form of marriage consists in this, that two become *"one flesh,"* (Genesis 2:24; Matthew 19:6)—but this is dissolved by adultery, for, the adulteress becomes one flesh with the adulterer (1 Corinthians 6:16)[2] and is no longer one flesh in individual society with her

---

1. The *"lege Julia"* or "Lex Julia" was first published under Julius Caesar in about 49 BC. Another lex, probably here referred to, was published under Augustus Caesar in 18 BC, which was chiefly concerned with marriage.

2. "What? Do you not know that he who is joined to a harlot is one body? For two, he says, shall be one flesh." 1 Corinthians 6:16.

husband. And so adultery absolutely breaks the bond or covenant of marriage. Therefore, how can men contend it to still be a bond when it is absolutely broken, or fancy a *"vinculum"*[1] that does not actually bind? And that adultery absolutely destroys all the forms of marriage will be granted. Therefore, adultery dissolves the bond of marriage itself.

Secondly, if the innocent party is not set at liberty upon a divorce, then:

1. He is deprived of his right by the sin of another; which is against the law of nature—and so, every wicked woman has it in her power to deprive her husband of his natural right.

2. In the case of adultery, that divorce, which is pointed to by our Savior for the innocent person to make use of, is, as all confess it to be, for his liberty, advantage, and relief. But on the supposition that he may not remarry, it would prove to be a snare and a yoke to him; for if from then on he does not have the gift of self-control, he is exposed to sin and judgment.

Thirdly, our blessed Savior gives express direction in the case: *"Whoever divorces his wife, except it be for fornication, and remarries another, commits adultery."* (Matthew 19:9). Hence it is evident, and it is the plain sense of the words, that he who divorces his wife for fornication and marries another does not commit adultery. Therefore, the bond of marriage in that case is dissolved and the person that divorces his wife is at liberty to remarry. While he denies divorce and remarriage for every cause, the exception of fornication allows both divorce and remarrying in that case. For

1. *vinculum:* Latin for 'bond.'

an exception always affirms the contrary to what is denied in the rule of which it is an exception of, or it denies what is affirmed in it in the case comprised in the exception. For every exception is a particular proposition contradictory to the general rule, so that when the one is affirmative, the other is negative and on the contrary. The rule here in general is affirmative: he that divorces his wife and marries another commits adultery. The exception is negative: but he that divorces his wife for fornication and marries another does not commit adultery. Or this may be otherwise conceived, so that the general rule is negative and the exception is affirmative: it is not lawful to divorce a wife and marry another; it is adultery. Then the exception is: it is lawful for a man to divorce his wife for fornication and marry another. And this is the nature of all such exceptions, as I could show in all sorts of instances.

It is to no purpose to except that the other evangelists (Mark 10:11-12, Luke 16:18) do not also express this exception; for:

1. It is recorded twice by Matthew (verses 5:32 and 19:9) and, therefore, was assuredly stated by our Savior.

2. It is a rule owned by all, that, where the same thing is reported by several evangelists, the briefer, shorter, more imperfect expressions of it, are to be measured and interpreted by the fuller and larger expressions of it. And, likewise, every general rule stated in any place is to be limited by an exception annexed to it in any one place whatsoever; and there is scarcely any general rule that does not admit some kind of exception.

It is even more vain to say that our Savior speaks only in respect to the Jews and what was or was not allowed among them; for:

1. In his answer the Savior reduces the laws of marriage to the law of creation and their primitive institution. He declares what the law of marriage was and the nature of that relationship antecedent to the law and institution of Moses; and so, reducing it to the law of nature, gives a rule directive to all mankind in this matter.

2. The Pharisees inquired of our Savior about such a divorce as was absolute—which gave liberty for remarriage after it; for they had never heard of any other type of divorce. The pretended separation *"a mensa et thoro"* only, was never heard of in the Old Testament. Now, if our Savior does not answer concerning the same divorce about which they inquired, but another which they knew nothing of, he does not answer them, but deludes them—they ask about one thing and he answers about another thing, answering nothing to their purpose. But this is not to be admitted, for, it would be blasphemy to imagine it. Wherefore, denying the causes of divorce which they permitted and asserting fornication to be a just cause for divorce, he allows, in that case, that kind of divorce which they inquired about, which was absolute and from the bond of marriage.

Again: the Apostle Paul expressly sets the party at liberty to remarry, who is maliciously and obstinately deserted, affirming that the Christian religion does not prejudice the natural right and privilege of men in such cases: *"If the unbelieving depart, let him depart. A brother or a sister is not under bondage in such cases."* (1 Corinthians 7:15). If a person obstinately departs, on pretence of religion or otherwise, and will no longer cohabit with a husband or wife, it is known that, by the law of nature and the usage of all nations, the deserted party is at liberty to remarry, because, without his or her default, all the ends of marriage are frustrated. Yet it may be that it is not so among Christians. What shall a brother or a sister that is a Christian do in this case, who is so departed from? The apostle says: "They are not in bondage, they are free—at liberty to marry again."

This is the steadfast doctrine of all Protestant churches in the world and it has had place in the government of these nations, for Queen Elizabeth was born during the life of Queen Katharine, from whom her father was divorced.[1]

FINIS

---

1. Queen Elizabeth I of England (1533-1603), a Protestant, was the daughter of Henry VIII (1491-1547) and his second wife, Anne Boleyn (1507-1536). Catherine of Aragon (1485-1536) was Henry's first wife and the mother of the Roman Catholic Queen Mary I (1516-1558) who ruled just prior to Elizabeth and earned the epithet "Bloody Mary" for her fierce persecution of the Protestants. It was under Elizabeth that England was firmly established in the Protestant religion.

"By manifestation of the truth commending ourselves to every man's conscience in the sight of God."
2 Corinthians 4:2

HAIL & FIRE

Hail & Fire is a resource for Reformed and Gospel
Theology in the works, exhortations, prayers,
and apologetics of those who have
maintained the Gospel and
expounded upon the
Scripture
as the Eternal Word of God
and the sole authority in Christian doctrine.

For the edification of those who hold the Gospel
in truth and for the examination of every
conscience, Hail & Fire reprints
and republishes, in print
and online,
Christian,
Puritan, Reformed
and Protestant sermons and
exhortative works; Protestant and
Catholic polemical and apologetical works;
Bibles histories, martyrologies, and eschatological works.

Visit us online: www.hailandfire.com

Made in the USA
Lexington, KY
16 September 2013